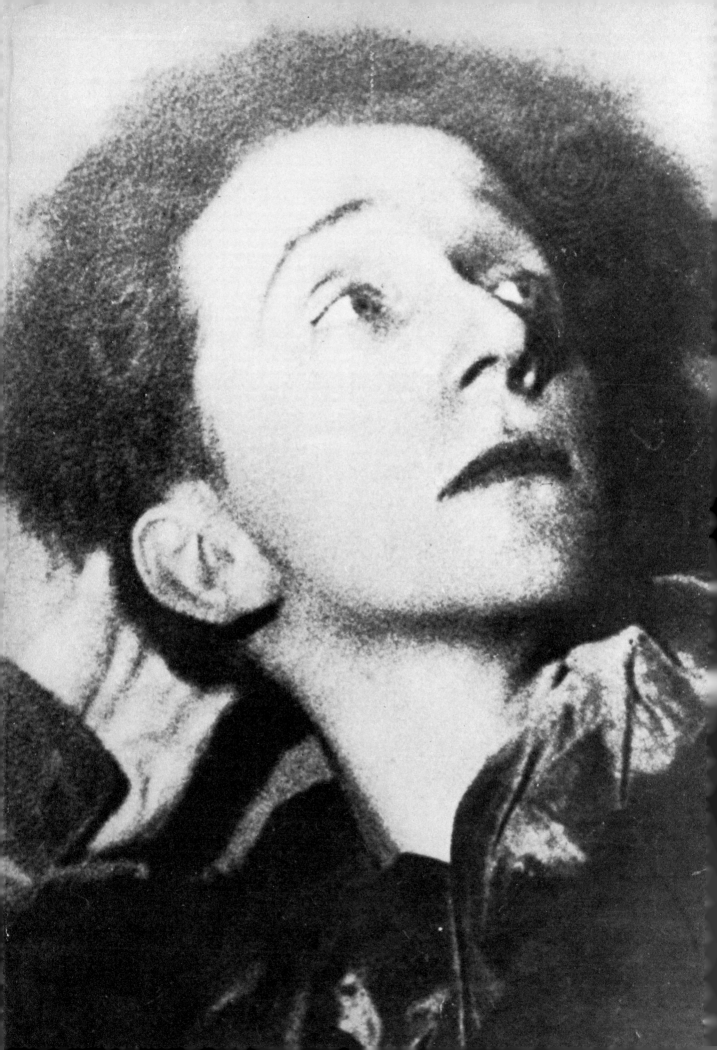

VICTOR ARWAS

ALASTAIR

Illustrator of Decadence

With 96 illustrations, 4 in colour

THAMES AND HUDSON

Half-title: Alastair's endpaper design for *The Sphinx* by Oscar Wilde (see pls 1–6).

Frontispiece: Alastair; undated photograph.

< Alice from *The Blind Bow-Boy* (see pls 39–40). Campaspe's sister, she appears to be the beautiful ideal of sweet young womanhood to Harold who marries her, and only then discovers her crass commercial soul.

Text and monochrome illustrations printed in Great Britain by BAS Printers Limited, Over Wallop, Hampshire

Colour illustrations printed in Great Britain by Balding and Mansell Limited, Wisbech, Cambs.

Bound in Great Britain

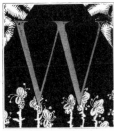HEN VERY YOUNG, Alastair set out to be an enigma. And succeeded. 'Who is Alastair?' wrote J. Lewis May in 1936. 'No one knows; not even — it is hinted — Alastair himself. But there are many rumours. One is that he has royal blood in his veins; some hot-headed Bavarian prince is supposed to have indulged in amorous dalliance with a pretty Irish girl, and Alastair is said to have been the offspring of this romantic but irregular union.' 'Alastair', wrote Robert Ross in 1914, 'claims to have Russian, Spanish and English blood in his veins.' To Alastair's delight he was referred to as German by English writers, as English by German writers, and as Hungarian by French writers.

Whoever his real parents were, Alastair was officially born in 1887 in Karlsruhe to a family named Von Voigt, the grandson of a lieutenant general stationed at Trier, in Moselle. He was later to claim he was a changeling: his official parents had received him immediately after his royal, though illegitimate birth, given him their name and brought him up as their own. There was certainly little if any resemblance or congruence of interests between him and his Von Voigt, Von Dassel and Von Ploetz relations, many of whom later accepted his explanation of his origins. Although he never altogether abandoned the use of his legal name, Hans Henning Voigt, or the title of Baron, which he mysteriously acquired, he chose to be known under another name, one that sounded vaguely mysterious, and English, and aristocratic: Alastair. He lived up to his chosen name in the way those people enraptured by the Aesthetic Movement had lived up to their blue-and-white porcelain.

Alastair received a good primary and secondary education, and was brought up to speak German, French and English faultlessly, with aristocratic accent and intonation. He wrote well and entertainingly, though he never learned to spell. He had exquisite manners, a rather precious presence and great artistic ambitions. He played the piano beautifully, frequently composing his own music. At the age of twelve he decided he wished to train as a dancer, and promptly joined a circus for a while, where he learned to move gracefully, and to mime.

After leaving school Alastair briefly studied philosophy at the University of Marburg under Professor Cohen, a neo-Kantian, and there met Boris Pasternak and Felix Noeggerath; the latter was to become an intimate friend and lover for several years. Alastair also spent a year doing anatomical and life drawings, but was so bored with the sterility of the teaching that he tore up all these drawings and began again from scratch, teaching himself, developing his own style.

The 1890s were his inspiration. Too young to have participated, he spent his early youth steeping himself in the atmosphere of *The Yellow Book*, reading Swinburne, Baudelaire and Wedekind. A mannered and theatrical young man, he exaggerated his mannerisms and theatricality, building — not donning — his persona.

He travelled throughout Germany, Austria, France and England, building a network of friends and acquaintances and, increasingly, admirers. He was nearly always a welcome guest because he was good value: spectacular and extravagant in looks and speech, witty and entertaining.

He met Baroness Elsie Deslandes in 1913, in Paris. A strange, virginal, though somewhat ageing creature she had, in her youth, inspired the writers Barrès and Bataille as well as the painter Forain with the chastest of passions. The Italian poet Gabriele d'Annunzio had promised to rape her in her coffin. She had written several novels, and had the curious habit of performing her intimate functions in an alabaster vase which her butler daily cleaned, then placed on a shelf in a living-room, filled with orchids.

At her home in 1914 Alastair performed one of his mime-dances accompanied by a young Russian sculptress and her lover and later husband, a cellist called Barjansky. Gabriele d'Annunzio, who was present, wrote in his notebook for *Notturno*: 'At Ilse's, around a Burmese golden unicorn, Alastair, dressed in an azure tunic brocaded with gold, performs gothic dances. The bronze deer seem to browse among the cushion-covers. A wax figure. A poet dressed as a bishop. The wind blows flames from the hearth into the room.'

The wax figure had been modelled by the Russian girl, Catherine. D'Annunzio, fascinated by Alastair, attracted by Catherine, organized several evenings throughout the year at which the two entertained. He would bring out a coffer filled with vials of perfume, and warm those scents he felt most appropriate to each succeeding piece of music or dance. Alastair, who had by now accumulated a vast wardrobe of exotic costumes, silks, brocades, velvets and chiffons, needed little encouragement to dress and perform, creating curious ritualized scenes which appeared to conjure up the supernatural. Several of d'Annunzio's mistresses and friends appeared, including the extraordinary Marchesa Casati, who lived in a Venetian palazzo, strolled through the streets with a pet ocelot on a leash, kept Afghan hounds and assorted lovers, courted scandal, organized magnificent balls and fascinated every artist and writer she met. La Casati ordered several macabre wax dolls from Catherine, including one of the ill-fated Marie Vetsera, the very young mistress of the Austrian heir to the throne, Archduke Rudolf, both of whom had been found dead in the hunting lodge at Mayerling. Alastair found in her the living embodiment of all those women he was creating on paper.

Untutored, therefore open to all influences, Alastair had taken Aubrey Beardsley's serpentine line and adapted it to his needs. Lightly outlining his characters, he filled in the details with solid areas and broken or dotted lines. He was fascinated by the rich patterns on fabrics: when able to afford them, he would order some from Fortuny, specially designed and dyed for him. In his drawings he contrasted large solid areas with painstakingly decorated ones. His use of colour was sparse, usually confined to a single colour in addition to, or in place of, black. Unlike the conventionalized features of Beardsley's drawings, Alastair's faces are tragic masks, eyebrows languishing downwards; wide, flat noses, wide, scarlet gashes for mouths.

All his drawings were either portraits or compositions inspired by novels, poems, plays or figures of legend or history. He drew Cleopatra and Salome over and over again. Oscar Wilde, Wedekind, Prosper Mérimée, Gustave Flaubert, Sardou, inspired sequences of drawings. Swinburne's poems inspired several – 'Our Lady of Pain' is a recurrent theme in Alastair's works, the sado-masochistic aspects reappearing in scenes of the Inquisition as well as in the evident delight he took in delineating the sufferings of Christ on the cross, though this may well be no more than an echo of the carvings in the Bavarian churches of his youth.

The portraits depicted friends, patrons and the sacred monsters of the stage. He drew Sarah Bernhardt and her great rival Eleonora Duse, who had long been d'Annunzio's mistress. He drew Polaire several times, emphasizing her curious,

almost skeletal, frame. Polaire, who came from Algeria, had been making a name for herself touring in the stage version of Colette's *Claudine* tales. He drew the young Mistinguett strutting with her walking stick. He drew an imaginary portrait of Paganini, the legendary violinist, whose incredible virtuosity had led to whispers of a pact with the devil: he was drawn bemedalled, playing his instrument while standing astride the recumbent body of one of his swooning admirers. He drew the Marchesa Casati more than once, but all his women echo her melodramatic features.

Maurice Magnus, a German-American writer with a penchant for helping artists, met Alastair through Count Harry Kessler, and introduced him to various people who might help him. Edward Gordon Craig, Ellen Terry's son and a great theatrical designer and theoretician, allowed his dislike of Magnus (who had in fact translated one of Craig's books into German and had often been of use to him) to colour the meeting: 'There was one Alastair whom Magnus took up – hooked up – with the intention of "running", . . . "helping". And there were several writers for whom he cast his line – Norman Douglas – D. H. Lawrence – Maria Martini – Jean-Jacques Olivier,' he wrote. Alastair he did bring to see me. I recall Alastair clearly. Whether Magnus actually came with him . . . no, now I remember, Magnus assuredly did *not* come: Magnus owed me some money and did not believe I would let him off; so Alastair was brought round by a friend of Magnus – one John Cournos, a Russian or a Pole.

It was 1912 or '13, in London – Long Acre – where I rented a warm but odd house.

Alastair arrived. They didn't carry him upstairs, but I felt he was frail enough for that. I did not know why he had come to see me. He seemed to be uninteresting – and not at all well – and not at all manly and not at all womanly – not charming – not handsome – not winning – not audible, and not much less than a bit of a nuisance.

I could see that Magnus would find him quite something to exploit, for Magnus took likings (and dislikings) if he saw what he thought to be money in it.

[II]

Alastair's meeting with John Lane was to lead to the foundation of his lasting reputation as an illustrator. Lane had started the Bodley Head in partnership with Elkin Matthews as a bookshop and publishing house. When their partnership was dissolved in 1894 after seven years the Bodley Head had already established itself as a leading publisher of aesthetic writing. Nearly all its books appeared in very limited editions, beautifully designed, frequently illustrated: its list of illustrators eventually included William Rothenstein, Walter Crane, William Strang, Robert Anning Bell, Laurence Housman, Charles Ricketts, Charles Shannon, Gleeson White, Selwyn Image, Wilson Steer and Maxfield Parrish. In 1894 Lane launched *The Yellow Book*, edited by Henry Harland and with Aubrey Beardsley as Art Editor. Attacked viciously by the reputable press, *The Yellow Book* became an instant success. Beardsley supplied many illustrations, often under pseudonyms: but when scandal broke over Oscar Wilde's second trial, Lane was forced to bow to an ultimatum from several of his leading authors and remove Beardsley from the magazine. This was ironical, since Beardsley did not even like Wilde. While Lane also withdrew all of Wilde's books from his lists and his bookshop, Beardsley joined Joseph Pennell and Arthur Symons to found *The Savoy*.

Beardsley still occasionally contributed to the Bodley Head after the break with *The Yellow Book*, and his relations with Lane remained of the friendliest, but the artist was extremely ill, and died in 1898 at the age of twenty-six. Lane saw another artist of Beardsley's originality in Alastair.

In 1914 John Lane published *Forty-Three Drawings by Alastair (with a note of Exclamation by Robert Ross)*. Issued in an edition of 500 copies through his London and New York offices, the book was bound in cream buckram with an Alastair drawing blocked in gold and with a further drawing on the endpapers. The illustrations, many in colour, were printed on one side of each page, interleaved with tissue paper printed with the titles. There were many individual drawings: portraits, designs for posters, illustrations of individual poems or short stories. In addition there were six illustrations for *Carmen* and seven for *Erdgeist* by Frank Wedekind. The introduction by Robert Ross, Oscar Wilde's last and best friend, gave some details of the artist. Alastair had, he wrote, 'a strong physique and radiant health. I cannot promise for him or collectors an early death: he is a total abstainer; and as he is only twenty four there is not very much to be said about his life or adventures.

He has had no training as a draughtsman, a circumstance dazzling enough to the ordinary observer but less so to the artist or the expert student, both of whom might have made the discovery for themselves. Alastair is one of those rare exceptions in whom the *atelier* might have strangled the individuality or dissipated the delicate fantasy of a wonderful invention. That he can now articulate forms with such extraordinary precision or can engineer elaborate designs without faltering must not, however, be taken as a precedent by those many 'geniuses' who can neither draw nor paint and who have

Marchesa Luisa Casati (see pl. 75).

dispensed with the ordinary discipline submitted to by Michel Angelo. That this young man should have formulated and perfected a style after only four or five years' experience is certainly very remarkable, and suggests to me that the peculiar manifestation of his talent is possibly a phase out of which something even more valuable may be evoked. The modern critics who search for rhythm and find it where its existence is a little doubtful must, however, be delighted to have heard already from the press, that Alastair is a musician and a dancer with professional ambitions. If these drawings are the expresssion only of a phase, they have an enormous psychological interest apart from their technical qualities. If they are the primitive fruit of a style 'in the making', they indicate the youthful hand of one who should figure at no distant date among the most remarkable personalities in European art.

The premature perfection of his art, the sophisticated placing of the figures, for example, on the paper (which the plates accurately reproduce) are, I admit, symptoms of precocious development if you take into consideration the age of the artist. I confess, indeed, to thinking it almost a fault that there is not more evidence of youth and experiment: there is something uncanny in the accomplishment. . . .

These drawings are significant not only as exquisite designs in an almost faultless technique, but as illustrations conforming to the ideals of book decoration existing before the naturalism and realism of the fifteenth century prevailed in European art. As illustrator Alastair has availed himself freely of the precedent set by Rossetti, embroidering and elaborating on his own account the text or the motive which he derives from some book or play. It would be interesting to learn if the distinguished dramatist Herr Wedekind is more pleased with some of Alastair's interpretations of his creations than Tennyson was with Rossetti's. Many of Alastair's 'caprices' are mere 'dancing on paper' and this group will appeal especially to those who resent all composition guilty of an idea. But I prefer the designs deliberately informed or inspired by some word or sentence that has fired the artist's imagination and quickened his power of invention, such as the *Carmen* sequence and the *Erdgeist* illustrations. . . .

His use of colour, however, it should be observed, though singularly happy, is restricted; there is no 'handling' or 'quality' therein. He employs it as an accessory for heightening effects or for relief. Though we should lose much by its absence, pigment is not, so far as I can see, essential to his peculiar method as it was for the Greek vase-painter, the medieval illuminator, or the Japanese printer from which he has gathered honey like a true eclectic. It is extraordinary that he should rival their achievements with fewer materials. . . . If Alastair could draw only well, he would have no interest for us. Drawing has long ceased to be even an accomplishment. It is because Alastair's drawing is nimble and expressive, and conveys a message however fantastic, that we must recognize and welcome his art. . . . Capacity and charm are drugs even in the English market. An artist must possess the idiosyncratic note, and we must be sure that he and his work, however derivative, have added to our aesthetic experience and aesthetic emotion, before we can accept him or trouble to consider his talent. This book prepared by Mr. John Lane affords I think a complete answer for those who doubt, and doubt naturally, the claims advanced on behalf of any new artist. Of recent years there have been so many sheep in wolves' clothing and Chelsea has become a veritable Val D'Arno.

Alastair's art is also quite untouched by the contemporary and, I believe, only temporary tendencies evinced by the later techniques of Matisse and Picasso, though the influence of those artists is wide-spread all over Europe. Such immunity appears to be an indication of strength and individuality, however much one may admire the new Byzantinism. The Cubists and the Futurists and the rest have passed him by: he has minded his own business. There is something pleasantly old-fashioned in his oddities and in the peculiar types he affects. New art which has permanent value and interest always combines the qualities of the seen and unforeseen. The fascination of Alastair's talent in its present manifestation is, I believe, permanent; perhaps his secret is *une modernité stylisée*, though, as I have hinted, that manifestation is not likely to remain an example of arrested development nor to wait for critics who apply the adjectives when it has been transfigured in the brilliant future of another avatar.

[III]

In 1914 Alastair met André Germain, with whom he was to have a stormy relationship for many years. Germain, a fairly wealthy young man about town, was to become a very prolific writer, on art, politics, literature and history; he wrote the first book on Renée

Vivien, the lesbian poet, in 1917, and wrote books on Goethe, Proust and d'Annunzio. His side of the relationship with Alastair was described in an autobiographical work, *La Bourgeoisie qui brule: Propos d'un Témoin 1890–1940* (The Burning Bourgeoisie: The account of a witness 1890–1940), published in Paris in 1951. Acknowledging that Alastair was 'an extraordinarily gifted artist' whose name meant 'fallen star', a name 'which fitted him, since there is in the name both dazzle and a great deal of melancholy', he wrote:

Alastair was a present to me from d'Annunzio. During that spring of 1914 during which I had the pleasure of frequently seeing the author of *Fire*, he enjoyed telling me about a young poet, artist and musician he wished me to meet. It was Alastair. We met one day in front of the poet's closed door. He was surrounded by a mixture of luxury and poverty which induced great pity in me.

He used to send women incredibly beautiful flowers, distributed royal tips to servants, and could not afford to pay his hotel bill. He travelled throughout Europe with a huge number of trunks containing the most magnificent clothes, but had no roof of his own. An air of splendour and decay hung around him. He always showed himself timid and extravagant, generous and frightened. And his chimerical attitude to life seemed to come not from a pose or from long acquaintance with Bohemianism, but from the sumptuous tragedy whose folds enveloped him.

He wrote, performed, sang and drew with a perfection surprising in one with such varied gifts. He also danced. Moving with a kind of effort hieratic costumes resembling chasubles, he executed, as though hypnotised, slow pantomimes which, stiffened with pride and pain, transposed sacerdotal wails and recreated the splendours of an exiled court. His long gestures, powered by Gothic despair, attested simultaneously to the line of Kings from which he believed himself descended and to some kind of God, both merciful and cruel, glimpsed through a glistening stained glass window. That, at any rate, was the way d'Annunzio saw him, and that is how I caught a glimpse of him under the poet's auspices on a curious evening whose memory has been fixed for ever in the *Notturno*.

Such traits of character predestined their possessor to exceptional artistic triumphs and to a great clumsiness towards life.

All this moved me to real pity. As Alastair, riddled with debts and tormented with the most varied worries, did not know where to turn, I invited him to the apartment I then occupied in the Avenue du Colonel-Bonnet. He spent about a fortnight there in July 1914 during which he never ceased to astonish me. He was at the same time chimerical and highly educated. He gave one the impression of emerging from a fairy-tale, but a rather 1890s fairy-tale, in which there was some Villiers de l'Isle-Adam as well as some Aubrey Beardsley, some aestheticism, some perfected liturgies, and a degree of witchcraft.

Where did this anachronistic being come from? He has covered his tracks to such an extent that one will never know. Nor will he. He was one of those who lose their key almost at once, or rather, one who throws his key to the sea.

Officially, he was the son of some very fine people, decorated with honours and titles, who had somehow sired him on the threshold of their old age. They had previously had daughters and sons who were in no way gifted or exceptional. How could the poetic disequilibrium of which Alastair is made have succeeded these normal offsprings? The mystery deepened the more one tried to grasp it. He himself explained it by affirming that he was a substituted child. A bizarre heredity, both Scandinavian and Spanish had, if one believed him, woven the complexity of his soul. When I met him his parents had been dead for some years. He no longer maintained any contact with his brothers and sisters. The friends of his youth – among them the highly intelligent Madame Andreae – have not been any more able to solve the problem for me. They too saw in Alastair a kind of princely vagabond who had apparently been, some years earlier, a very elegant young man, rather worldly, thrilling at the piano, and perfect in his choice of ties. Elegance had gradually given way to extravagance, and worldly statelessness to a kind of sombre nostalgia.

Alastair had gone back to Munich in July to perform some of his dances, but the outbreak of war had interrupted his season, and he had fled to Switzerland. Germain saw him briefly again in October 1914, but it was not until 1916 that he returned to Geneva, accompanied by the elderly Mlle de Larnage, who was to become a close friend. He and Alastair were to spend the next four years together in Switzerland, though their relationship then and later was to be punctuated with explosive breaks and reconciliations: Alastair never believed in lying diplomatically, and held to both honesty and analysis with a firmness that was often cruel. Germain's account of their relationship is a curious mixture of admiration and hatred, and was obviously written with a great deal of resentment still smouldering years after it had ended. Alastair was very hurt when he read it, but there is little doubt that his own candid observations had, throughout his life, hurt those who could not take such honesty.

When I rejoined him in February 1916 [Germain's account continues], he was more lost than ever. During those eighteen months he had known various dramas – real or imaginary – wandered from city to city, met some honourable professors. He was like the ivy: seeking a place to cling. A temporary life gradually organized itself around me, in which Alastair and Mlle de Larnage were the bizarrely joined poles.

It took them some time to understand each other. After being presented to Mlle de Larnage, Alastair sent her a bouquet of admirable violets, which were a tribute to her severe looks and almost canonical age. Yet these violets were, by a kind of symbolic coquetry, topped with a little flame, a single and shining red ranunculus.

In truth Alastair and Mlle de Larnage soon loved each other. They both had an equal and constant need of the pathetic which occasionally sparked one against the other, but usually brought them together. They both had a taste for emotions and the gift of tears. At first I tried to shape myself to this rhythm: I was soon exhausted. I then fought to give them what they did not want: peace.

Alastair was always ready to create sentimental imbroglios. He had for this purpose a full kit box of fairly brilliant women, very thin, very aesthetic, highly educated and totally unbalanced. The first was Lilith, a somewhat Jewish Russian of great beauty who – though she had tormented several men to death – appeared the picture of innocence.

The most interesting of the men who had perished through Lilith was a young German archaeologist from a remarkable, though absent-minded family. At the time of his suicide – accomplished from the top of a Corsican rock – his whole family had gone on a trip, forgetting to leave a forwarding address. Various alarming telegrams brought no results. At last she who did not know herself to be a widow received a telegram containing only the words: 'What do we do with the coffin?' At first she did not know whose coffin. When she finally realized her loss, she recited two hundred verses of an ancient tragedy, applicable to the circumstances, and since she was most erudite, she recited them in Greek. She then persuaded herself that she ought to seek and welcome the involuntary murderess. Which she did. Since Lilith had no more roof than Alastair – they had, in fact, lived together for a few months – she accepted the widow's hospitality. Both women went into mourning, and remained very close for the rest of their lives.

Despite her picturesqueness and her adventures, Lilith was a bore beyond expression. Alastair, who rarely noticed the boredom that was communicated by his beautiful admirers, suddenly noticed Lilith's boredom. It was a catastrophe. . . . As an epilogue to so many flowers sent and so many love letters exchanged they wrote each other the most dreadful business letters concerning a sum of money she had once lent the artist. Alastair eventually paid the debt, but the bouquets did not flower anew.

Gabrielle succeeded Lilith. She was less pretty, but far more gifted. She was prodigiously thin, dressed with elegance and extravagance, recited verse, wrote. She was, of course, misunderstood. She had a husband, a talented critic, whom she often divorced and generally remarried. She too had herself baptised. Despite her gifts and her complications she too, unfortunately, was extremely boring.

Although she remained for many years Alastair's official Muse, he soon gave her rivals. First came Loulou. Loulou, whom I have since known well, then derived great glory from her affair with Germany's greatest poet, Rilke. She was prodigiously pale, with fine hollowed features and stormy hair. Short-sighted and slightly lame, she walked shakily, as though in a dream. And she was prodigiously absent minded. Suddenly Rilke, who had been her most patient and attentive friend, stopped replying to her letters. He did worse: he stopped opening them. She was shattered by this, which she could not understand. On the other hand, impetuous in her correspondence, she bombarded her own sister with more than vehement letters of reproach. 'You whom I have always hated', she wrote to her.

After Rilke died all her letters, which the poet had piously kept unopened, were returned to her. The last letter he had opened began with the words: 'You whom I have always hated. . . .' Poor Loulou had put the letter in the wrong envelope. She understood at last the reason for her disgrace.

In the autumn of 1917 Alastair, having learned that Loulou was ill in a Zurich clinic, wrote to her: 'Madame, I know you hate me, but I send you flowers.' The usual magnificent flowers accompanied the letter. Loulou was charmed. Meetings took place, all wrapped in mystery. A correspondence began which, seeing the literary quality of the two writers, must have been of great quality. But Loulou and Gabrielle met in the antechamber of Alastair's sick-room and there was a pulling of hair. To mortify Gabrielle, Loulou pretended to take her for a young man.

Alastair later pretended that Loulou was becoming dangerous because she was engaged to a Kaffir King who was particularly dangerous from an occult point of view. He used this as an excuse to break with her.

There then appeared the greatest woman poet of Germany, Else Lasker-Schüler. Alastair, always worried and changing his address, was then living with one of my friends, a Dutchwoman of great merit, an artist and poet. . . . One day the charming woman was visited by Else Lasker-Schüler, whom she did not know. The latter showed her a photograph and said: 'I found the image of this young man on the floor of the railway station. I was utterly moved. I have been looking for him ever since. Intuition told me I would find him here.' After this direct speech the poetess was introduced to the artist who was languishing on a sofa. Nothing much followed: some letters and some flowers.

The latest arrival was Bianca. She was, outwardly, the most singular. She carried, over her magnificent body, a head that must once have been marvellous, but which had long ago turned sharp and menacing. Dressed as a witch she would have had considerable success on the stage, where she had always dreamed of going. Dark and with sparkling eyes she looked like the Devil's widow.

She, too, was unfortunately extremely boring. And she was not merely an oral bore, but an epistolary one. If one was unfortunate enough to be introduced to her she would promptly shower you with letters, the slightest of which stretched over twenty-four pages. She put down her hopes and loves on paper.

Bianca only interrupted the monotony of her idyll with Alastair by suicide. At six o'clock one morning the groom of her hotel, which was next to ours, woke Mlle de Larnage: 'Madame is very ill and Madame is asking for Mademoiselle. Madame has just committed suicide.'

Mlle de Larnage hurriedly put on some clothes and went over. She found Bianca in bed, her magnificent black hair — her finest feature — artistically laid out, hugging to her bosom a bunch of red carnations. The contrast of dark hair and scarlet flowers was, I am told,

very effective. Mlle de Larnage worried at first at the state of the sick woman who indicated with a gesture that she could no longer speak. She was, however, reassured when she noted that the deadly liquid the suicide had just swallowed was . . . a bottle of Vichy water. Of all the Alastairian loves Bianca's suicide was the most violent episode.

These tragedies, simultaneously inoffensive and boring, but which borrowed some fairly aesthetic aspects from the faces of their heroines, lacked the proper setting. For they nearly always took place in hotel rooms, comfortable of course, but sadly ugly. The innumerable flowers with which Alastair surrounded himself, and the animal skins he threw over the furniture, were not enough to create an atmosphere. And yet many times, in fantasy or reality, some magical settings had been improvised.

In 1916 I wanted to buy the very small, but very beautiful castle Gümmligen, just outside Berne. I was attracted to it by the ghost of a beautiful dead woman. The Duchesse de Polignac had stayed at Gümmligen in 1789, at the start of her exile; and the exquisite dwelling had remained as in the days of the young Duchesse, powdered. It was a most reasonable price. Yet to buy it I needed, because of certain family arrangements, my brother-in-law Fabre-Luce's permission. He was despotic and disliked the arts, so he refused it.

I have since often regretted it, for Alastair, who had infinite good taste, would undoubtedly have made a marvel of Gümmligen. He had already attached himself in thought to the little house as to a beloved he wished to cover in lace. In order to redeem his lost dream I tried to create for him a home that would be entirely his. But he was as thirsty for a house as he was incapable of staying in it.

He had, in fact, found a three-room flat on the corner of a mediocre street in Zurich whose Empire decoration – swans and cupids – was absolutely intact. It was a masterpiece which only needed to be cleaned and set off. Which is what Alastair did. He settled in triumphantly, yet three months later he moved out saying that the looks of his neighbours – two old maids – displeased him.

I let myself in for another, equally vain attempt at setting up house. The wandering artist had, this time, chosen a kind of owl's nest at the foot of a huge mass of limestone in Lausanne. Its humidity was terrifying. Alastair only consented to notice this after lining all the walls of his future home with sumptuous fabrics. He then fled abruptly, with not a single backward glance at those walls he had so ardently coveted. Chased by some demons or ghosts, he always fled.

What I forgot to mention was that those years, crossed as they were with amorous agitation, had been, for Alastair, years of incessant creation. Work led this disordered being to the most severe discipline. Rising at six o'clock in the morning he hardly ever went out, but filled his day with a huge programme. Gymnastic exercises which preserved the dancer; piano exercises which perfected the musician; study of his singing; the most diverse literary occupations from those, like letters and poetry, which suggest fugitive inspiration, to those – translations especially – which demanded the maximum

The artist at home.

application and perseverance; and drawings, multiple drawings which are witness of a heart-rending imagination in the faces and of the art of a consummate and ingenious embroiderer in the clothes of the characters: all of this in succession did not weigh down an organism which yet was particularly sensitive and fragile. And there were some fine, some admirable gifts in all this. The gift of language in particular was developed to extreme perfection in Alastair. The least shade of French words was meaningful to him. You felt it when he read aloud to you from Flaubert, Huysmans and Alain-Fournier, who were among his favourite authors; you also noticed it in the highly coloured letters, in the exquisite poems he wrote in our language. And music was, for him, a kind of extended language in which the most profound part of his being expressed itself, in which his perpetual nostalgia exploded in heart-rending accents.

One felt that nothing he attempted brought him any closer to his real life, neither his chimerical loves, which soon became irritating, nor the friendships which his sickly touchiness soon led him to break, nor the beautiful objects he surrounded himself with, which he loved and never learned to keep and which, having brightened up his exile for a while, soon vanished at the pawnbrokers or in some disastrous sale. His real life was lived at the piano.

His gifts, so numerous and brilliant, were unable to earn him a living. His artistic gifts were tainted with the same misfortune as the wealth of his soul; nothing was adapted to his times. Twenty years earlier, when Beardsley triumphed, Alastair might well have become highly fashionable. But he came too late, and although it was still fashionable to patronize the mediocre heirs of the English artist, this fashion did not extend to Alastair, who was so greatly superior to all those vulgarizers. He was, in any case, singularly maladroit in his dealings with critics, impresarios and editors, all those awkward screens through which blows fame.

In any case, all his soul's energies were applied to feeding his perpetual unhappiness. Some friends showed astonishing zeal in fighting this unhappiness. An admirable artist, Renata Borgatti, was one of his most devoted ones. But none of his friends succeeded in overcoming the curse which, fathered by him or renewed through circumstance, pushed him under for ever. To tame him would perhaps have been less paradoxical than to console him. In that hope I sent him to a famous tamer of souls, Mme Le Fer de la Mothe. Having loved each other from a distance with a kind of intuitive passion, they quarrelled when close together, without bearing fruit. Nothing could force open the gates of the prison in which he locked himself up. He did not know how to love; he did not know how to pray. Friendship laid its sincere offerings to him in vain; he was hurt and irritated by what should have appeased him. How could

God have entered his cell crammed with flowers and overburdened with perfumes? The pain with which he lived was not for him the preparation for his divine visit: he was unable to make his heart kneel.

Rather than be understood and consoled, he was eager to dazzle himself with I know not what vain incantation. He seemed to be for ever listening to the siren's voice which kept repeating the wonder of his unhappiness. Where is he wandering now? For to him all is disappointment and exile. Only an angel could reason with him; but do angels still come to us? From the human side there is no hope for him. Good will — and there was a great deal of it directed towards him — invariably failed. And it let him fall, even sadder, to his vain and dazzling fairyland, to the calls and images of his insatiable inner gulf.

Alastair had a great gift for friendship. Throughout his life people were attracted to him. The bizarre aspects of his outer persona undoubtedly contributed to this attraction, but much more was needed to hold those who were attracted. He was an incomparable raconteur, clever, amusing; a gifted musician, singer, dancer, mime, composer; but he was very demanding. Imperative in his needs, not overly grateful when his needs or demands were fulfilled, he was not an easy recipient of favours. He did not suffer fools, and frequently dissected other people's pretensions with surgical skill. When he lost interest in someone he would discuss that person sharply and with no excessive diplomacy. Yet he kept some friendships close and alive throughout his life. Separation of years made little difference to those, which were renewed whenever possible.

Shortly after his arrival in Switzerland Alastair contributed seven drawings to a curious little volume called *Poèmes pour Pâques* (Poems for Easter) by Loïs Cendré. This was a slim collection of short verses printed privately in Geneva in March 1915 in a very limited edition and distributed by Cendré to his friends as an Easter present. Alastair's drawings are among his most Symbolist, and were printed in black on a beige paper, with parts of the drawings silk-screened in gold and white. The drawings were, however, contributed anonymously: the book stated that the seven drawings were by 'Celui qui aime l'amour' (He who loves love).

The relationship with André Germain lasted throughout the war years in Switzerland, but continued on and off for a further dozen years. Germain went on giving Alastair money whenever he needed it. In the post-war inflationary years in Germany Alastair was suddenly well-off, since he had foreign currency from Germain. It enabled him to rent part of a Bavarian hunting lodge in the grounds of Schloss Lustheim, a castle near Schleissheim. Part of the lodge housed a great German porcelain collection, and Alastair delighted in the fact that the place was haunted. He finally broke off with Germain at the end of 1929.

[IV]

The publication of *The Sphinx* in 1920 signalled the start of Alastair's decade of fame. The book had been planned before the war. The illustrations had been printed in Belgium and stored in London during the war years: as a note in the book pointed out, 'This edition is limited to 1,000 copies and cannot be reprinted, as the stones from which the offset plates were printed were in Belgium at the time of the German invasion, and were destroyed.' There were ten full-page illustrations, eight different ornamental letter designs, two different endpaper drawings and a cover design blocked in gold and blue on the white buckram binding. All the illustrations were printed in black and turquoise.

Oscar Wilde's poems had inspired some of Alastair's most effective drawings: chic, decadent deities such as Ashtaroth with towering bee-hive hairdo, twin-hooped skirt and fan, encrusted with pearls, twin breasts gleaming, heavy-lidded eyes emphasized by twin blue heart-shaped beauty spots; or Isis and Osiris, a triangular unity whose act of homage is more a fusing; Antinous, a dancing youth leaping over the barge rail, he and it bedecked with flowers; a blue Nereid in her element, seaweed-encrusted body curving backward to form a capital C, her black hair curving in the opposite direction to echo that C; Apis, a caparisoned and befeathered black bull; Pasht, 'who had green beryls for her eyes', a mass of embroidered fabrics overlaid to form an overwhelming frame for a tiny, wizened face; and a crucifixion, which Arthur Symons was later to describe as the

vision of an emaciated Christ, whose eyes are half-closed: it is a marvellous and symbolic representation of Christ's last agony on the Cross, and there is pity and wonder in it, for there is no cross and his hands are nailed, but upon no wood. . . . Alastair's Christ hangs in mid-air against a night as black as Hell and his feet are not visible. I have rarely seen a more beautifully painted Christ: the pure outlines of that divine body, the locks of black hair matted with sweat that falls down on both sides of his face: the ghastly sense of death in those half-closed eyes, the eyelids not yet fallen over them, the mouth wide open after its last gasp — and it has been said and Blake believed in it that the Soul escapes through the mouth. The anguish expressed on that dead face is unutterable. Only one who is Catholic in spirit could have achieved this masterpiece.

Other books and sets of illustrations appeared. Alastair illustrated Prosper Mérimée's *Carmen* for the Verlag Rascher in Zurich. A small volume reprinting Wilde's *Salome* in the original French was printed in December 1924 by G. Crès in Paris with nine illustrations by Alastair. In the United States he illustrated Carl Van Vechten's *The Blind Bow-Boy*, while Barbey d'Aurevilly's tale *La Vengeance d'une Femme* was published with Alastair's illustrations under the title of *Die Rache einer Frau* in Vienna.

The Blind Bow-Boy enabled Alastair to return to the depiction of the androgynous male. He had already drawn 'that young god, the Tyrian, who was more amorous than the dove of Ashtaroth' for *The Sphinx*. Naked but for a loincloth, the Tyrian exemplified the ambiguity of Alastair's creatures: he could be a flat-chested girl. Van Vechten's novel allowed Alastair to depict a contemporary Tyrian. The god of love, the Bow-Boy himself, is a pretty, breastless Diana. 'Harold' in his tight suit, two-tone shoes, hat, gloves and cane; and 'Ronald' in sailor suit with floppy beret, on the other hand, are the quintessential effeminate dandies, sexually uncertain yet clearly attractive. They are what Joséphin Péladan, the archpriest of nineties decadence and the Rosicrucians, called 'the intangible Eros, the uranian Eros'.

Few of Alastair's women show any androgynous aspects. Unlike so many late-Victorian nudes, they are not men with breasts, but real, if theatrical, women. In *The Blind Bow-Boy* the women are prettier, less tormented than is usual in Alastair, and the contemporary setting allows him to essay a variety of clothing. 'Alice', holding a bouquet, wears a floral dress; 'Fannie', in black and grey velvet, is swathed in lovingly delineated furs; camp 'Campaspe', hair cut short and curled, wears an off-the-shoulder pearl-encrusted dress with a feather stole forming wings curled round her body.

[v]

Alastair had met Austin Osman Spare through John Lane, who had financed a new quarterly publication called *Form*, edited by Spare and Francis Marsden. The first issue had appeared in April 1916. Lane had hoped it would be a new *Yellow Book*, but it proved to be more a vehicle for Spare's writings and illustrations. It was not financially successful and the magazine soon vanished when Spare joined the army, where he redesigned, wrote for, and illustrated the *Royal Army Medical Corps Magazine*. An abortive attempt to revive *Form* was made in October 1921, when a second series was attempted in a slightly smaller

format edited by Spare and W. H. Davies. Published by the Morland Press, which had printed the original magazine, it was intended as a monthly publication but did not survive.

In October 1922 the first issue of *The Golden Hind*, edited by Clifford Bax and Spare, appeared, published by Chapman and Hall with a distinguished if small list of subscribers. It was full of drawings, lithographs and woodcuts by Spare and John Austen, as well as Robert Gibbings, Laurence Bradshaw, Ludovic Rodo (Pissarro), Haydn Mackey, Glyn Philpot and several others. One drawing was listed as by 'V Voigt Alastair', a simple line drawing of an ephebe. The fourth issue, published in July 1923, contained two drawings by Alastair, whose name was here published simply as 'Alastair'. The first of these was an early variant of his *Queen of the Night* drawings inspired by Mozart's *Magic Flute*, while the second was a not very successful drawing of a woman in a long black cloak, which covered part of her face, balancing a vase on her head from which floral garlands drooped all over her. Both drawings were fairly poorly reproduced, and lost much of their impact by their small size.

Spare influenced Alastair more through his verbal than his artistic talents: though he was a magnificent draughtsman, his inspiration was too different from Alastair's. Spare was involved in magic and the supernatural, was a magus and was engaged on research into the unconscious inspirations of art. One of the first artists to experiment with automatic drawing, he frequently created monstrous beings and blasphemous conjunctions of great power.

Alastair had long been interested in mysticism and self-exploration. Most of Spare's complicated jargon did not, however, appeal to him, so he simplified the ideas to a basic opposition of good and evil characterized as angels and devils inhabiting every human being. Spare's theories on automatic drawing, developed with Frederick Carter, were more attractive to Alastair. 'Out of the flesh of our mothers come dreams and memories of the gods', they had written. Rejecting literal reproductions as 'not more than slightly useful', they recommended 'an "automatic" scribble of twisting and interlacing lines' to allow 'the germ of ideal in the subconscious mind to express, or at least suggest itself to the consciousness. From the mass of procreative shapes, full of fallacy, a feeble embryo of idea may be selected and trained by the artist to full growth and power. By these means, may the profoundest depths of memory be drawn upon and the springs of instinct tapped.' Alastair became an instant convert to the technique, yet he was unable to confine himself to the doodle, invariably turning out exquisitely finished drawings. His literary tastes were, in any case, so pronounced that his usual heroines and victims emerged time and time again from his preliminary doodles, further convincing him that his role in art was to re-create those sacred monsters of history and romance, a task he set to with panache.

In 1923 Alastair published a curious little piece of writing in a luxurious German fashion and literary magazine called *Styl*, published in Berlin by the Verlag Otto von Holten. 'Die Verwandlungen des Dandy' (The Metamorphosis of the Dandy) was an attempt at universalizing what he had long felt about himself and his destiny, linking this with his love of the past. 'To be called rightly a dandy demands more than to ensure merely that the gleam on the toecaps of one's boots are utterly without a speck', he wrote.

A dandy cannot emerge from a pack of backward cretins; for in order to achieve an immaculate outer appearance, one needs an inner attitude based on mental attributes beyond those condemned to the superficial. The true dandy is in control of every situation in his life. His generosity and courage are taken to extremes, while his outer attitude is always utterly unconcerned; he is unbusinesslike – not through stupidity but from choice – for under no circumstances is he prepared to reveal his feelings. Above all, while both the hero and the villain may adopt the persona of the dandy, neither can do so if not fated or fortuitously. It is a disguise created by heavenly women on bended knees who watch over the fate of fragile humanity with motherly care in order to protect their beloved ones. It is a mask making its way through the constantly changing, tawdry finery of the world with its pulverised centuries of error and intrigue. Its classic disguise emerges from the carnival in Venice; a chalk-white monkey face frozen over the lace frills of silken capes which enable their wearers to join secret orders.

A dandy is not the outcome of choice but an accident of birth; his status cannot be achieved through effort but only through fate. The most genuine embodiment of the concept may well have died at the very moment the image was conceived, just as its most exquisite prototype may have lived before recognition. In the ancient world there was equal merit in being beautiful or wise, each of those states being recognized as different paths to perfection, similar in their relationships to that between mathematics and music, mathematics being the abstract form of irrevocable creation in music.

From the pyramids of dancing Egypt, where even the tiniest expression of life was devoted to sacred and meaningful systems, the dandy emerged. He knew that there were insoluble enigmas and that peaceful harmony determined the course of life and death, even in its phantom rebirth. The dandy could be found among the death-defying heroes, the fighters for freedom in Greece,

with a jest on his lips as golden Nike lifted him from blood and death to join the immortals on wings of laurel. Crowned with a wreath of distinction he relaxed nonchalantly at the feet of philosophers at a banquet: he was as well known in places of learning and of civilization as in the echoing marble surroundings of the theatre. The dandy sat at porphyry tables as the aloof partner in perfidious games with irate emperors to whom Rome and the world knelt in the dust. Emerging from the bath immaculately clad he omitted to pay homage to effigies of the insane potentates, even if those very colossi passed by in their shaky litters dripping with pearls. In Chinese bell-encrusted pagodas the dandy wrote verses perfumed with irises, remaining unembarrassed when hysterical princesses on tinkling porcelain bridges posed health-damaging questions. The Samourai dandy sacrificed his life in wistaria bowers for his fierce ideals, sure in the safety of tradition; with not the slightest desire to share his thoughts, he smiled in the face of the most jagged fate so that through his superiority the demons would never be certain of victory. . . . He tossed yellow carnations onto the stakes of the Spanish Inquisition and stood in the shadows of the complex intrigues of the Italian Renaissance while papal courtesans played to him on the harp. The dandy slept dreamlessly through the terrors of St. Bartholomew's night and rescued black and white in the religious wars; he waved fans with dragonfly iridescence in the torchlit sarabands in the gardens of St. Cloud and manipulated foil and poison in the northern courts. He exchanged letters in French with the ill-treated heirs to the Prussian throne, handed over his treasure of diamonds to fashionable alchemists and embarrassed notorious actresses on the river Thames. In the darkness of revolutionary dungeons the dandy tapped minuettes and gavottes with his dying red heels and, when the tumbril to the guillotine called, he went on distributing with perfect manners to powderless duch-esses the cards of an interrupted game. Nor did he fail to beg the executioner's pardon should he accidently knock his elbow. He drifted around Napoleonic battles and waited outside a famous singer's house for years in a chequered carriage. He put on cardinals' hats and Czarist crowns, fools' caps and anemone wreaths. He . . . but enough! The dandy has appeared throughout history with the smooth, nonchalant movements characteristic of his name. It is superfluous to list the names of famous dandies – they are no doubt familiar to the sufficiently cultivated reader, from Alcibiades to Montesquieu, from Amenophis IV to Alexander the first and the pitiable Brummell. Only this still needs to be said: the nearer to our times the more doubtful the dandy, and I think it is probable that the historical genius who dwells in a grotto with stalactites is wrong in his comments and frequently repeats categorically what has never been true. Significant for the recent past is the appearance of so many literary figures disguised as dandies, hardly believable since deep consciousness must overshadow the purity of the case. And that one, much despised and overpraised as he was, could never have been a dandy through the blood line – otherwise he would not have suffered what did happen to him, and would have met his fate in a different manner.

The publication of this article heralded a parallel writing career. He published a number of translations into French of poems by Henry von Heiseler and Stefan George in *La Revue Européenne*, which also published some of his original poems written in French. One of his close friends was Ludwig Derleth, a member of Stefan George's circle. He published some of his German poetry in a magazine called *Horen* and, in 1920, published a volume of it in Munich. Entitled *Das Flammende Tal*, it was published by the Hyperion Verlag. Throughout his life he also devoted much time to translating novels, collected letters and other works, some of which were published anonymously.

[VI]

In the years that followed Alastair continued to work feverishly, executing hundreds of drawings, many of which he would destroy. Each image was worked out in his mind and in sketches, so that several variations exist of specific images. In 1925 he was given an important exhibition in New York at the Weyhe Gallery which opened on 26 October, closing on 7 November. Dr Charles Fleischer reviewed it in the 31 October issue of *The Art News*:

The mysterious Alastair is represented by a group of drawings at the Weyhe Gallery. Probably curiosity is particularly piqued by the fact that Alastair chooses to hide his identity. But the distinctly individualized quality of his work would be bound to provoke an interest in the personality of its creator.

Characterized as the greatest living master of his chosen field, Alastair certainly fascinates you with the sheer beauty of his drawings, their intricate design, their bizarre conceptions, their sardonic temper, their decadent spirit. Frequently, as if in fiendish mockery of humanity, the detailed loveliness of gowns or of settings puts into painful contrast a face intrinsically ugly in its viciousness or distorted in a grimace of suffering.

As it happens the show at Weyhe's opens concurrently with the publication (Alfred Knopf, publisher) of a book of Alastair drawings. In his introduction, Carl Van Vechten calls attention to the fact that, whereas Alastair is an illustrator (the present series illustrates Van Vechten's *Blind Bow-Boy*, Wedekind's *Erdgeist*, *Salome*, *The Temptation of St. Anthony*, *Camille*, etc), so original is Alastair's genius that the artist's esoteric fancy frequently leads him far afield from the source of his original inspiration. Therefore, too, the resulting designs are confusingly distinct from the influence acknowledged in his titles. For instance, says Van Vechten of the *Tosca* drawings, 'whereas play and opera smell of vulgarity,' Alastair's

illustrations 'are expressive of a limpidly refined depravity'. . . . There, for instance, is Alastair's *Salome and Jochanon*, a sex-dripping draping of the voluptuous, lusting woman against the austere, agonized loathing of the doomed prophet. And next to it, *The Death of Salome*, in her final throes still hugging the severed head of her belusted John.

Alastair runs to allegory. He likes to depict Pride in all her silly vanity of beauty; Anger again in beauty, but terrible, dripping blood in showers from his uplifted hands; Death embracing Life, eclipsed by his black figure. In fact all his even historical or dramatic themes are lifted by the genius of Alastair out of the merely personal and individual into the region of the allegorical where they become universalized in their human implications and applications.

Not stimulating, inspiring, or even pleasing are these drawings but they have the fascinating beauty of menacing orchids or of the gorgeous scum on the surface of a stagnant pool.

The book sold well; the drawings less well. Van Vechten's introduction pointed out that when Alastair's first book was published by John Lane in London,

he was a mysterious figure of twenty-four, trailing behind him certain clouds of glory from the 'nineties. Now, eleven years later, surer of his touch, more master of his own personality, he still remains a mysterious figure. From the security of a seventeenth-century Bavarian hunting lodge, occasionally he has sent a few of his delicate designs out into the world, but he himself has preserved his seclusion. His remote art, then, utterly uninfluenced by contemporary tendencies, not concerning itself in the least with current movements, is actually the embodiment of his strange personality. In reflecting upon the names of modern artists, I can recall only two even superficially his kin, Gustave Moreau and Aubrey Beardsley. His resemblance to these men, however, is much more a matter of temperament than a matter of influence.

A tortured, perverse, morbid temperament, informed with a bitter sensitiveness and a divine pity! Even in such a rococo bit as the sketch of Manon Lescaut, the face of the Chevalier des Grieux exposes the essential irony of existence as it has been experienced by Alastair, while the skirt dancer from *Erdgeist* is Death itself lifting flowered petticoats with a measured gesture of frivolous despair. Nothing would be more expressive of the essential futility of life than these puppets, save the puppets of Aldous Huxley, with whose ineffectual and decadent attitudes the drawings of Alastair bear a well-defined affinity.

This attitude of mind may appeal to some, may be repulsive to others; what saves it from sheer austerity is the beauty of the detail, the baroque over-elaboration of which is an individual idiosyncrasy, the unerring sense of design, the exquisite and reserved employment of colour for emphasis; these things are done lovingly and suggest a warmth of treatment which may attract those repelled by the sardonic, though illusively poetic, imagination of the painter. There is a curious paradox to

15

be noted here, in an artist who lavishes all the beauty at his command on the robe of Herodias, while he withholds it from her face, who gratifies our sense of grace with the gestures and habiliments of Marguerite Gautier, while he terrifies us with the suffering in her expression. It is quite possible, however, that it is through this paradox that the aloof Alastair betrays his instinctive sympathy with our restless, pathetic, modern life.

The Bavarian hunting lodge Van Vechten had mentioned was Schloss Lustheim.

Alastair returned to London, then Paris, reshaping new exhibitions, replacing sold drawings with new ones on the same themes. In London he frequently stayed with the John Lanes, who were very fond of him. In his biography of John Lane, J. Lewis May quotes from a letter Alastair wrote to Mrs Lane, thanking her for replying to a letter he had written to her husband:

Thank you so much. The black Madonna will smile to you – because you like to have her under your roof. There exists quite a number of black Saints – especially black images of the Holy Virgin. Some of these are blackened by age or fire. But the more important ones have always been black. Few people know why. Many reasons have been given. The true reason is – the glory of the suns cannot be painted. The glorious features of the Madonna therefore have been represented eaten up by blackness. Like the brightness is hidden by blackness if you look at it too long. Ten days ago, I went to an arch-old chapel near Fuysing in Bavaria, consecrated to one of the most curious Saints of the Catholic church: Die heilige Kummernis – holy sorrow, a woman with a gilded beard. The truth is the great goddess Astarte or Ashtaroth is hidden under the changed name and attitude of 'holy sorrow'. Do you remember the charming legend of the danseur de Notre-Dame? The original Saint was not the virgin, but 'holy sorrow,' who dropped the jewelled slipper. What a lovely time you must have had up in Scotland.

This letter clarifies a curious aspect of some of the drawings he executed of Sarah Bernhardt, the Divine Sarah, in which he drew the little fur collar she often wore, but treated as though it were a beard. He must have been making the connection with 'holy sorrow', the woman with the gilded beard, Sarah being the modern incarnation of Ashtaroth.

He retained a life long admiration for Sarah. Although he only met her a few times, he saw her perform in a number of plays, and invariably defended her as the greatest actress of her time, placing her far higher than Eleonora Duse, whom he knew better, or any of her other rivals, French, Italian or German.

'The glory of the suns', he wrote, 'cannot be painted.' He was soon to meet a man obsessed with the sun, a man who would have a major part to play

in his life. Alastair had taken a house in Versailles at 19 rue de Lafayette, and soon had an exhibition organized in Paris.

[VII]

The private view took place on 4 February 1927. Alastair held court. The guests vied with each other in the extravagance of dress and compliments. Alastair himself stood dramatically swathed in his velvet cape, occasionally flicking it open to reveal flashes of his silk moiré suit. It was here that the Duchesse de la Salle introduced two guests she had brought with her to Alastair, a young American couple, Harry and Caresse Crosby.

Harry Crosby was a young man with a death-wish tempered by enormous energy, a burning desire to experience everything and a powerful, though undirected, creative urge. Born to a wealthy Boston family with strong banking connections, he was both nephew and godson of J. P. Morgan. A few days after graduating from school in 1917 he had sailed for France, there to enlist as a volunteer in the American Field Service Ambulance Corps. He was later to join the US Army as a private, but was promptly put in its ambulance section. He both drove ambulances and carried the wounded in several battles, narrowly avoiding death at Verdun when his ambulance was destroyed by shell fire: the narrow escape from death was to form the cornerstone of the rationale of his later decision to take his own life. Shortly before returning to America after the ending of the war he was awarded the Croix de Guerre.

In 1919 the twenty-one year old Crosby went to Harvard College, where he was eventually awarded a shorter War Degree. During his second year as an undergraduate Crosby met Mary Peabody in Boston. Born Mary Phelps Jacob, she was six years older than him, and had been married in 1915. Her husband had given her two children in between going to war in Mexico and then in France, but was spending the post-war years as an amiable drunk. Crosby fascinated Mary (known as Polly), soon seduced her, and insisted violently on marrying her. He fought with her, with his family, with hers, threatened suicide if she refused him. Harry joined a Boston Bank after leaving Harvard, but spent most of his time drinking, and left after only a few months there. His father and uncle got him a job at Morgan, Harjes & Co in Paris. Polly followed him there, but the relationship proved too stormy for her and she sailed back to New York, hotly pursued by young Crosby. In the midst of scandal Peabody had given his wife the divorce she wanted. In September 1922 she and Harry were married in New York, returning to Paris almost immediately afterwards. 'We can become very cultured and improve ourselves', he had written to her.

In June 1923 the Crosbys moved out of their Hotel and took a flat on the Île Saint-Louis. He made occasional token appearances at the Morgan Bank, which paid him a small salary, but he spent much of his time drinking, partying, going to the races, pursuing pretty girls. Three months later they moved to Princess Marthe Bibesco's apartment in the Faubourg Saint-Germain. In November Harry Crosby first met Walter Van Rensselaer Berry, his father's cousin. Born in Paris in 1859, Berry had studied at Harvard and at Columbia University, where he had taken a law degree. In Washington he became an International Lawyer, before moving to Cairo in 1908, where he was appointed a Judge at the Tribunal Mixte (International Court). He had returned to France in 1911, had been influential in bringing the United States into the war, and had been president of the American Chamber of Commerce in Paris since 1916. He had never married, though he had had several mistresses. Edith Wharton, the novelist, loved him, and he had directed and shaped her talent. His friends came from both the literary and the aristocratic world: Marcel Proust had dedicated *Pastiches et Mélanges* to him. Louis Auchincloss, in his biography of Edith Wharton, quoted Lady Ribblesdale's verdict: 'Unlike some gentleman callers who left their hostess with a baby, Berry left them with a book.' He liked the Crosbys, and took them under his wing, inviting them repeatedly to meet such diverse people as Jean Cocteau, Paul Valéry, the Duchess of Marlborough (the former Consuelo Vanderbilt) and Marshal Foch.

Harry Crosby wanted to write poetry. Berry encouraged him, opened his library to him, set him reading Baudelaire, Rimbaud and Verlaine. At his cousin's prompting, Crosby left the Bank. In December 1924 the Crosbys decided that Polly needed a new and more euphonious name: they eventually settled on Caresse. A few months later Harry and Caresse each had a slim volume of poetry published, for which Harry paid. Determined to pursue a life of decadence, they travelled to North Africa, where they smoked hashish and took a thirteen year old Berber girl dancer to bed. Harry also began to smoke opium, and had the soles of his feet tattooed with crosses. He was already obsessed with the sun. Writing in his diary, parts of which were to be published at various times under the general title of *Shadows of the Sun,* Harry described

the little Berber dancer with her 'matchless breasts like succulent fruit', ending, 'O God when shall we ever cast off the chains of New England?' Back in Paris Harry added a fourteen year old American girl, whom he dubbed 'Nubile', to his growing collection of mistresses, with all of whom he claimed to be in love. In November 1925 the Crosbys moved to 19 rue de Lille. They went on travelling, met Ernest Hemingway and Archibald MacLeish while skiing at Gstaad, organized mad costume parties and orgied at the Bal des Quat'z'arts.

Alastair appeared to Harry to be the embodiment of all his fantasies, a creator of the most outrageous fancies who was also, himself, an outrageous creation. Harry wrote to his mother that 'he couldn't sleep all night', and soon arranged to be invited to Alastair's home in Versailles. Many years later Caresse described that first visit: 'He lived in a sort of Fall of the House of Usher house, you know, with bleak, hideous trees drooping around the doors and windows – we always suspected him of having them trimmed to look that way – and he had several blackamoors for servants. On the night when we came first to see him, a blackamoor ushered us into a room where there was a black piano with a single candle burning on it. Soon Alastair himself appeared in the doorway in a white satin suit; he bowed, did a flying split and slid across the polished floor to stop at my feet, where he looked up and said, "Ah, Mrs. Crosby!"'

Their friendship soon blossomed. Harry travelled south to Saint Paul de Vence, between Antibes and Nice, where Alastair had a studio 'looking out over the battlements towards the sea', and bought some drawings. Six weeks after their first meeting Alastair was writing to Harry: 'No death begotten sadness has killed the clearsight of your goodwill. You have played with the demons but they have not been able to destroy you – for love's sake. . . . it is very strange but when I just saw you both – Mrs. Crosby and you – in the big gloomy room – it seemed to me like something that happened before.' Alastair basked in their admiration: Harry described Alastair in a letter to his mother as 'exactly like what Shelley must have been – and the *only* person I have ever seen that expresses my idea of genius'. In return he appeared as their star turn at dinner parties and soirées, and invited Harry's mother, who was visiting Paris, to tea (with a well-contrived mise-en-scène.) 'Your mother perhaps would think me dreadful', he wrote. 'But if it would cool an afternoon for you, have tea with her chez moi and I'll sing for you, be anything you imagine.' A little later he wrote: 'If I put on a house garment 17 is your mother going to think I am a lost soul?' Harry soon realized that despite the hired servants, the incense and the silks Alastair 'hasn't a sou' and he began giving him small gifts.

Shortly after meeting Alastair the Crosbys discovered a small printer in the rue Cardinale, Roger Lescaret. They liked his work, and impulsively decided to start their own publishing house, whose offices they set up on the upper floors of Lescaret's shop. It was to be called Editions Narcisse, after their whippet, Narcisse Noir, for whom they were later to buy a companion whom they named Clytoris. Narcisse Noir accompanied them everywhere, his toenails lacquered gold, his collar encrusted with diamonds. Alastair called him the 'well behaved black wave'.

One of the first books the Crosbys published under the Narcisse imprint was *Red Skeletons*, a group of poems by Harry, illustrated by Alastair. The poems were dedicated to Alastair in an envoi which read:

> *I see*
> *Against the moon*
> *Four lines crucified*
> *Which are the four thoughts that I have*
> *Of you.*

Headed by brief quotations from Oscar Wilde and Baudelaire, the volume consisted of short poems derived from Baudelaire and Swinburne which attempted to re-create the drug-obsessed whiff of decadence with titles like *Red Burial, Black Sarcophagus, Futility, Désespoir, Coeur Damné, Temple de la Douleur, Orchidaceous, Dance in a Madhouse, Necrophile, Unfertilized* and *Uncoffined.* Harry's poetic talent was only infrequently capable of coping with his overheated images. The opening poem, *Symbolique*, began:

> *Within the strange menagerie of my brain*
> *Fantastic figures fornicate and fuse*
> *Into deciduous monsters that abuse*
> *The girl-gold visions over whom I reign*

They were very much a young man's attempt at verbal intoxication, with occasional success. Arthur Symons found in them 'a strange orig-inality, something macabre, violent, abnormal, sinister, and also – "shadows hot from hell".' Alastair produced nine drawings, printed in black and sanguine, which are among his most successful. The frontispiece was *Our Lady of Pain*, a subject he had interpreted several times already since reading Swinburne's poem. Symons called this image 'a wonderful reincarnation of the cruel and ghastly divinity'. *Salammbô* was an extraordinary floral extravaganza of woman with cobra, while *Cleopatra* was one of his hieratic women framed in lotus flowers. Harry's poem *Crucifixtion* was illustrated with Alastair's least sanguine version, which emphasized the theatrical and stylized gestures of grief of the three Marys.

Only 370 copies of the book were printed, many of which were given away to friends of the Crosbys. Alastair dedicated one copy 'in true admiration' to Yvette Guilbert, the realist singer who had inspired some of Toulouse-Lautrec's most famous images. She had been in retirement for several years when the couturier Paul Poiret, whose pre-war fame and fortune had been dwindling, decided to launch a nightclub, called L'Oasis, in the garden of his home. He had a huge inflated balloon-like umbrella anchored to float above the trees to protect the guests from any inclemency in the weather, and devoted one season to re-creating the 1890s in atmosphere and décor. The cabaret consisted of singers made up and dressed to look like some of the great stars of the nineties, singing their songs. Poiret managed to persuade Guilbert to come out of retirement and the act began with an imitation on stage soon interrupted by the real Yvette Guilbert, who would stand up in the middle of the audience and exclaim: 'No miss, your interpretation is very sweet but not right. This is how Yvette Guilbert sang' – and she would launch into song. Her season at L'Oasis revived the legend, and was one of Poiret's few later successes.

After that brief season she attempted various ventures which were close to her heart, though with little popular appeal. She attempted to restage French medieval mystery plays as well as the earthier comic farces and romances. Closest to her was an attempt to revive the forgotten treasures of French chanson, from the lays of trouvères and troubadours to those of the sixteenth to the nineteenth centuries. Alastair had met her through Eleonora Duse, who was a close friend of hers. He was to accompany her on the piano at several soirées at the homes of various distinguished people. These recitals were received with a fair degree of enthusiasm, but the ones held in theatres never attracted the public until she agreed to return to her old repertoire of nineties songs, which meant a popular season every year. In 1927 she had also taken the role of a sinister speculator in Marcel L'Herbier's film *L'Argent* (Money), based on Emile Zola's novel updated to take in Art Deco settings and jewellery designed by Paul Templier.

Alastair was still in touch with his London publisher, although John Lane himself had died in 1925. 'The Manon drawings have been taken by the John Lane people,' he wrote to Harry, 'edition de luxe ready next autumn – this fall they are publishing an English edition of Sebastian van Storck by W. Pater. I have been doing many new designs.' The Pater book had first been published in a German translation with Alastair's drawings by the Im Avalun Verlag in Vienna in 1924. The John Lane edition, co-published in New York by Dodd Mead & Co, had a new introduction by P. G. Konody, in which he wrote:

whether, like Walter Pater, Alastair is destined to influence his contemporaries in art, it is perhaps too early as yet to say. He is still a fairly young man; and if he has already arrived at a degree of experience and a perfection of technique that many artists better known to the public may envy, no one can say what future developments his art may undergo. ... Like Lindbergh upon his monoplane venturing alone across the Atlantic, Alastair has flown upon his pen the whole breadth of human emotions, and in so doing he has led the way that others may follow. The greatness of the feat does not appear at first: the very brilliance of the achievement makes it look simple – half-a-dozen illustrations to an essay by Walter Pater – but think again; read between the lines of Pater and look between the lines of Alastair's figures, and every time you will see new depths of meaning, greater subtleties of interpretation – in a word, the genius of line illustration which even dramatic performance could hardly improve or expand.

[VIII]

In January 1928 Editions Narcisse published Edgar Allen Poe's *The Fall of the House of Usher* in an edition totalling 308 copies, with five drawings by Alastair and an introduction by Arthur Symons. Two hundred and fifty copies were sold in the United States by Edward Weeks, an editor of *The Atlantic Monthly*. Weeks had suggested to the Crosbys that Symons should write the introduction, and it was the second Symons introduction of an Alastair book to be published in 1928. Alastair's drawings for this book were a complete break with his usual technique. Abandoning precise outlines, he provided five lead-pencil drawings, all in shades of grey and black with only a very few, sparse, touches of red pencil.

There is a strange linear imagination in Alastair's designs for the rectangular vault in which Madeline was buried [wrote Arthur Symons], the vast arches, the sense of space, the flood of intense rays, ghostly white and slightly stained with touches of red, red as blood, issuing from the iron door. Here and there this creator of mystery strikes one's arrested senses, striking straight at the nerves of delight. A wild and exquisite imagination builds up shadowy structures which seem to have arisen by some strange hazard and to the sound of an unfamiliar music,

and which are often – as in the case of Poe's fantastically inhuman verses, as also in the case of Alastair, who shares the inhumanity of Poe ... literally like music in the cadence of their design. All have vastness, dignity, remoteness; a sense of mystery which becomes morbid, an actual emotion in their lines and faint colours.

The ghastly heads of Usher and Madeline (between whom sympathies of a scarcely intelligible nature had always existed) have on them the wan pallor of death; the heads pressed close together, Usher, with his masses of tangled hair, has closed his eyes, the wild eyes of Madeline are wide open, foreseeing death: and over their heads, with subtle malice, a spider has spun its delicate web, and the threads intersect these two faces. The ghastly pallor of the skin is accentuated by this gossamer texture. .... The apparition of the emaciated Madeline, cadaverously wan, is a masterpiece. Behind her one imagines a crushing force which weighs on her like a great weight, something external and horrible, something that suggests madness and the chimera's power over the mind and over the soul. Here, then, as in other designs, we have a kind of abstract spiritual corruption, revealed in beautiful form: sin transfigured by beauty. And here is an art in which evil purifies itself by its own intensity, and by the beauty that transfigures it. ... Alastair, who claims to have Russian and Spanish blood in his veins, and who has something exotic and mysterious about him, translates many of his pictures into another language, which they speak, with a fascinating foreign accent. And then, there is his genius.

Dissatisfied with the name of their publishing company, the Crosbys changed it to 'At The Sign Of The Sundial', under which they published Harry's book *Chariot Of The Sun*. This name, too, did not please them, and they changed it again to the Black Sun Press, the name that was to endure. Alastair wanted to illustrate another Oscar Wilde tale, and the Crosbys published *The Birthday of the Infanta* in two versions, one in English and one in French. Harry Crosby himself wrote the introduction in his usual heated style, admiring Alastair's 'diabolic beauty', defining him in the words 'infinitely secret and apart is the genius that has torn the heart from the black swan of beauty to offer it to some cool and mirror-like, infinitely delicate, infinitely secret sun which he has never chosen to unveil.'

Harry Crosby's diary recorded on 10 June: 'Alastair for luncheon and he arrived bearing the most marriageable looking lilies and our Black Sun Press is going to edit *The Birthday of the Infanta* with nine of his drawings and hardly an hour after he had left a bookseller from New York whom we had never heard of before appeared and bought from us the entire edition of the *The Birthday of the Infanta* but is this any more of a coincidence than the coincidence before luncheon when I went up to the library to get my copy of Chariot of the Sun and found the long gold finger of the sun touching the very centre of the Sun engraved on the book which was lying on the table near the window?'

Harry's love-affair with Baudelairian decadence did not last long. He was beginning to admire contemporary writers, was in correspondence with D. H. Lawrence, talking James Joyce into letting him publish some of his work, had joined the Editorial Board of *transition*, was planning an edition of the forty-seven unpublished letters from Marcel Proust to Walter Berry. Berry had named Harry as his residuary legatee. He had also stated Edith Wharton should have first choice of the books in his library and that Harry should have the rest. No sooner had Berry died than Harry conducted a veritable battle with Edith Wharton whom he accused of trying to take over the whole library. Though she was entitled to it she was eventually brow-beaten into taking seventy-three books or sets. Harry got the rest, a priceless library of over eight-thousand rare volumes, which he soon began to get rid of: he would leave the house with a sackful of books which he would give away to taxi drivers and barmen, or leave casually on the stands of booksellers on the banks of the Seine.

Shortly after publishing *Red Skeletons* Harry had written to his mother, 'you will be glad to know that it is my swan-song to the decadent', but it was not until 1929 that his hatred of these poems erupted in a characteristically violent act. He collected every copy he could find, a total of eighty-four, took them to Ermenonville, where he and Caresse had rented a mill-house, fired repeatedly at the pile of books with a shotgun, and set fire to them, dancing wildly around the pire.

Harry's fascination with Alastair was also dwindling. In the early months of their friendship Alastair had basked in his new friend's admiration, and soon came to depend completely on him. 'I need a friend – no – I need you – because your demons do not frighten my angel and because I begin to know you better than you know yourself and because you are not only able to hold your own tongue but perhaps the tongue of others', he wrote to Harry in September 1927. Harry was both friend and patron. Yet the element of novelty in Alastair which had originally attracted Harry soon palled because he expected the artist to remain a mysterious decadent wraith to be summoned only when required to enliven the occasional dinner party. Alastair certainly fulfilled this allotted role whenever required, appearing on such occasions dutifully dressed entirely in black, his pallid face a tragic mask, swooning from time to time. There was, however, more. Alastair wrote letters

continually to Harry, sent him poems, needed his approval and friendship in a way that embarrassed Harry. Harry's domestic entanglements seemed always directed towards complicated relationships – preferably women who were married, or engaged to be married. Although at least partly bisexual, since he is known to have slept with an Arab boy, Harry drew away from the romantic element of the emotional flirtation Alastair needed. By April 1928 Alastair was writing to Harry: 'Something in you is afraid of me. Why??? I know you ever so much better than you know me Harry. You do not even look at me – but the other way – I am sad that you did not tell me you disliked the . . . drawings. Other people told me. You wrote me other things. Why? It was unfriendly Harry and it hurt me.'

It was not that Harry disliked the drawings, but merely that he habitually made fun of things, frequently denigrating that which he most admired or coveted. He was also perfectly conscious of the fact that it was Alastair's drawings that had brought his publications whatever fame or notoriety they had. Harry resented this in an obscure way because it changed their relationship, which he liked to think of as generous Harry helping out poor Alastair. Alastair knew his worth and expected to be properly paid for the work he submitted; this, too, irritated Harry.

Manon Lescaut was published by John Lane in 1928 with a fulsome introduction by Arthur Symons which Alastair described as 'music to my ears'. There was talk of another book to be illustrated by Alastair for the following season. It was to be *Hamlet* or *Peer Gynt*, the choice to be made by their American correspondent, but the spread of the Depression quashed the idea. Alastair wrote to Caresse: 'I would be very grateful if you told me quite frankly if or if not you want to have work of mine for books. Please tell me quite frankly dear Caresse – and without fearing to hurt me – anger me etc. etc. I do not want to bother you with details of my life which surely do not interest you – but it is much too important for me to know something definite. If you do not really want to continue to work with me – say so. Otherwise let me do for instance Hamlet for the 15th of June. Ten drawings and two endpapers.' When Caresse told him she was travelling back to the United States, he wrote her: 'If the bookshops ask, offer for instance City of Dreadful Night (of course) – Hamlet – Macbeth – Peer Gynt – La Dame aux Camélias – Le Diable Amoureux (Cazotte) – Temptation of St. Anthony (Flaubert) – Les Diaboliques (Barbey d'Aurevilly) – Gaspard de la Nuit (Aloysius Bertrand) – delicious and free besides – books by

Selma Lagerlöf – Hamsun – plays by Strindberg and Wedekind.'

During 1929 there was a dramatic shift of style in the books published by the Black Sun Press. They included James Joyce's *Tales Told Of Shem And Shaun*, D. H. Lawrence's *The Escaped Cock*, *The Bridge* by Hart Crane, *Einstein* by Archibald MacLeish and Kay Boyle's *Short Stories*. Relations between Alastair and the Crosbys were rapidly deteriorating. Caresse told Alastair she needed some drawings urgently, and would send a car to collect them in the early morning. Alastair worked all night to complete the drawings, but no car arrived. He was hurt and furious. 'Please do not act like that – I do not accept it from my friends', he wrote to her. 'I am grieved and must tell you so. I do not think there is ever any reason for acting unkindly.'

In December 1929 the Crosbys published the last book to be illustrated by Alastair for them: *Les Liaisons Dangereuses* (Dangerous Acquaintances) by Choderlos de Laclos. The reason for the publication was a new translation of the work by Ernest Dowson, and they produced it in a handsome two-volume set in an edition of 1005 plus 15 copies on Japon paper each with one of Alastair's original drawings. Alastair had not realized this, and wrote to Caresse: 'Are you going to change the translation? *Please inform me – if so* – Because if – why not take the extremely well done old translation who even has the advantage of being free and of no cost therefor – it would certainly be quite unnecessary to do a new one besides everybody would grow old and diminish –'.

[IX]

Alastair's relationship with Caresse Crosby had become surprisingly close. His letters to Harry were frequently replied to by Caresse, who sent him some of her poems. Alastair's letters soon addressed themselves to both Harry and Caresse, then largely to Caresse alone. 'Oh Caresse,' he wrote her from Houdemont, a small village near Nancy where he was spending a holiday, 'but I do want so much to be human and angelic and a reality not a shadow. You did smack me but I love you very much for it.' He even revealed a little jealousy. Harry and Caresse were very close to Franz and May de Geetere, a couple of rather Bohemian artists living on a barge moored on the Seine. 'Of course that charming Dutch lady could not help it,' he wrote to Caresse. 'The watercolour drawing I mean. Is she fond of you? It is not you. Not here and there. You say you like it? Please don't.' Referring to a portrait of Harry

by Polya Chentoff, one of Harry's many lovers, he wrote: 'I cannot understand any more quite clearly that you care for the drawings out of mine – if I see the sad picture of the probably charming Polya Ch. . . . How can you pretend to love the sun or call that a sun picture? . . . (I do not even believe P.Ch. to be charming because if she was she would do you otherwise or recognize she did unreal things).'

When Caresse asked him if he liked the country, he replied: 'I never ask myself. In a way it is quite the same to me where I am now. The inner landscape makes the outer. Happiness or unhappiness. I build my country like spiders do. And the ugly and the plain lands are sometimes softer to me because there is more to add to them of the garden of Paradise.' Another letter ends: 'I read and read your last poem. It is so much nearer to yourself. Very gifted indeed, dear Caresse. I am extremely fond of it. Please think nicely of me and be aware of the thought that comes from Hanaël.' Once the initial reserve between them had broken down he signed all his letters to the Crosbys, 'Hanaël', a name he reserved for his closest friends. Shortly after meeting Harry's mother he wrote to Caresse: 'Caresse – why did you say the other day I did not care for the melodious image? If I did not care for it, certainly I would have gracefully said so. Be sure. Cause I am really a friend and not a diplomatic institution – Only you see – a very heavy cupboard has fallen on me so my gestures are not altogether easy – natural or my own. I hope Mrs. Crosby did not think me too quaint – I thought she was delightful and strange – Never forget that I am certainly twice as shy as you.'

Most of his letters are penned 'in haste'. Many of them reveal his obsession with ill-health. 'It is impossible to sleep and to eat – impossible just now to come to Paris. Because I faint all of a sudden and people drag me into chemist shops and drench my tie with brandy.' In the country in summer months, 'It is so hot that all the small remains of my brain are shrivelled, withered and gone. . . . A horrible fowl begins to gurgle in the twilight – they call it nightingale – but it is not true – it gives me hystero-nauseatic fits.' He ends a letter 'gibbering with neurasthenia.' Another: 'I am having an attack of something – fever and little disgusts – I tried to make believe it was not true – but it did not work.'

His obsessive secrecy about his antecedents recurred throughout his life: he referred to himself as 'the thing in the iron mask'. In a letter to Caresse he wrote: 'Caresse – yesterday I was afraid because you mentioned the red hair. Very few of my even real friends know. Do never please say anything about it. It would certainly be just the wrong person. Oh Caresse – I hate to be vague – but you cannot realise

21

what it is like to be always unfree and in moral chains. Between the devil and the deep sea. You can not know what it is like to be continually masqued as somebody else – to meet a stranger in the looking glass – to live apart of your native quarter. That is why I am so often not at all sure of myself. In the house it is better – I am less fettered and closed up there – but only few degrees less.' The letter ended dramatically: 'destroy this letter *at once* please.'

He frequently advised the Crosbys on details of interior decoration, and designed some dresses for Caresse, as well as discussing, often seriously, the most infinitessimal sartorial detail with her. 'Not lemon for the coat – dear,' he wrote to her; 'I do not think it goes with your colouring – rather *extremely pale* powder pink or pale orange running into rose and lined with gold lamé under faded pink crèpe georgette or chiffon. Lemon is only becoming for very pale people or brown.' Again, discussing her 'smoking' or evening dress, he wrote: 'Your smoking, dear lady with the hopeful feat, is rapidly becoming an angelic silver armour – I have seen you in a dress – an evening dress of lizard skin – with a garland of metal – tinted leather flowers and crystal leaves and a transparent cloak of old Spanish silver lace over topaz gauze – in your hands a moon-shade of the dust on gold brown feathers of the bird the cat ate yesterday. I do not know its name. It says affected things at midnight.'

[X]

A major exhibition of Alastair's drawings had been held in Paris at the Galerie Jean Charpentier in the Faubourg Saint-Honoré from 11 to 29 December, 1927. There were drawings for *Carmen, Red Skeletons, The Temptation of St Anthony, The Fall of the House of Usher, The Picture of Dorian Gray* and *La Vengeance d'une Femme*, as well as imaginary portraits of Paganini and Gaspard (i.e. Kaspar) Hauser and a few other drawings. The catalogues had two introductions, one by the Comtesse de Noailles, a distinguished poet, the other by Arthur Symons. 'It is with that facility which is the very nature of inspiration – that divine secret – that that admirable artist, Alastair, establishes the mysterious labyrinth of his compositions in which Ariadne's thread, that fine black cord, similar no doubt to the nocturnal tint of Grecian urns, hurls itself, gathers itself, circulates, winds and unwinds', wrote Anna de Noailles.

The eye follows with delight that clever, thick or aerial embroidery, funereal and springlike. For Alastair's marvellous gift is never as perfect as when the butterfly joys of a Japanese flowering mix with the tragic. . . . Within each sheet the tragic torture, I would even say the obsessive Shakespearian grimace, expands or contracts within tufts and garlands of roses. Juxtaposition of the black angel of evil and the considered and adroit ingenuity of the conscious, though wholly pure, Virgin; mixture in the witch's cup of the dark essence of henbane and the angelic balm of the white hyacinth; brutal marriage of anxiety, of the knifed heart, of the last gasp, of the unadmitted crime and the flounced nymph, of tenderness and an astonishment filled with pity, these are the hard and concise poems wrapped in celestial grace which Alastair delivers from his private dreams and inscribes on paper. Thought is as seduced as immediate vision, and invaded by the mysterious talent of this remarkable artist inhabited by the demanding dream people, all craving life.

Alastair had an exhibition in Brussels the following year at Eddy's Art Studio in the Place du Châtelain. It was opened on 16 March, and lasted to the 31st, and included drawings for *Manon Lescaut, The Blind Bow-Boy, The Temptation of St Anthony, The Magic Flute* and *Salome*. The catalogue reprinted the Comtesse de Noailles' text, and pointed out that Alastair drew portraits, designed costumes and furnished interiors.

[XI]

Alastair always had a friend to depend on. For much of the twenties it was Maurice Bayen. Alastair's frequent visits to the outskirts of Nancy were solely to be close to Bayen, whose family lived there. Bayen travelled extensively, but Alastair was not always able to follow him. In a letter to Caresse, Alastair, whose spelling was invariably atrocious, made a deliciously Freudian slip: 'I cannot *bare* the absences of Maurice Bayen who is a perfect friend and who always succeeds in tempering my anguish.' When Bayen travelled to Istanbul and Alastair was left behind, he complained plaintively that Bayen 'was my protection against dark things'. He went to the South of France, then on to Switzerland ('I do not mind the mountains'), but in the end could not resist and joined Bayen in Istanbul. 'What am I to do,' he wrote. 'Romantic lifes are so uncomfortable.'

Years later, in 1966, Alastair wrote to Caresse mostly about the war and post-war years:

My life continued to be quite awful and quite wonderful. Formerly you did not quite realise what happened to me – for even then I foresaw the approaching horrors – Maurice B. saved my life twice – he is a kind of anima Candida and therefore I was his. He is a sort of minister now in France – for university questions and educational transformations and international exchange. He has a charming wife and five children. So many of the English and Paris friends have passed to the next room (I hate to say dead – because it is not the exact word – it says the body where only the outworn coat is in question), Mme de Noailles – her sister Chimay – Renée de Brimont – Armande de Polignac – Mme de Chabannes – Mercedes de Gournay – Jean Rouvier etc. etc. . . .

He was still in Turkey when the news of Harry Crosby's suicide reached him. Expected for tea with Caresse and his mother at J. P. Morgan's, after which they were to join Hart Crane for dinner and a visit to the theatre, Harry had instead taken one of his most intense mistresses, Josephine Bigelow, to a friend's studio and had there shot her before shooting himself. It was 10 December 1929. On 3 January 1930, Alastair wrote: 'Caresse – Caresse – Caresse – there are no words. Paris people wrote to me what happened. I could not believe it. Dear heart – why can't I come to you and be with you in silence – be in song – it is impossible to realize that Harry has gone so far away. And so very much on his own account and without saying goodbye. . . . There *are* objective laws of existence – bigger than our will and wonder. Oh be sure. And if you think of the Divine forces – of Love – for Love is God – do not think of state rules, of silly priests and crumbling churches.' Lamenting his inability to be with her, he wrote: 'But I am quite poor at the moment – (I had to tell André G. that I could not regard him anymore as a friend and so could not accept his help any more. He is my enemy poor thing – This between us).'

On his return to Paris he found a present from Caresse, a mounted bust of himself, and was 'perfectly overwhelmed to find myself so beautiful.' 'Too poor to send you flowers,' he wrote, 'but they are always in my heart and hands for you.' Correspondence between them became desultory, but he insisted that all drawings she held of his were hers. 'Burn those you dislike and keep the others – if there are any left.' Indeed, he frequently destroyed his own drawings.

[XII]

The 1930s were a difficult decade for Alastair, as for so many. There was little demand for his work, and he travelled throughout Europe visiting his friends. Much of the time was spent in Switzerland with his close friends Robert Faesi, professor of literature and author of several historical novels, and his wife, the beautiful Jenny Faesi, whom Alastair teased as the 'femme fatale de Zurich'. Alastair would seek his inspiration indoors while Robert Faesi would take his rhyming dictionary into the garden. He was also close to Rathenau's daughter, Edith André, whose husband was one of the founders of the I. G. Farben complex, and he visited Carl Friedrich Freiherr von Weizsäcker, one of Heidegger's leading disciples and head of the Max Planck Institute. He frequently accompanied Pablo Casals and Alfred Cortot on the piano, and found himself playing two-piano pieces with the mathematician Heisenberg in Berlin, an experience he later described as 'musical torture'.

There was no demand for expensive limited editions of illustrated books, so he sold drawings or sets of drawings whenever he could. Offering a set to Frank House in New York, he wrote:

They belong to a book of the mystic Francis Thompson: The City Of The Dreadful Night. Originally they were made for a friend of mine Harry Crosby – the nephew of Morgan – who had five or six books made with my drawings. Before this suite was forwarded to him I lived in Constantinople, at that time he died in a tragic way. It was impossible for me to use these designs for a European edition as the author is not much known here. And in America or England only an edition de luxe could have been arranged and this is at the moment very difficult. I could give you these drawings for a very fair prize.

In 1939 he was staying with Mrs Arthur Schnitzler in Berlin, down to his last penny. Friends organized a scheme by which each would take one of his drawings every year, paying for it at the rate of one pound or twenty marks per month. 'If you know someone who would join in this giddy enterprise – please tell me', he wrote Caresse. 'And do not hate me for bothering you with this.'

He was in Switzerland when war was declared, though Nazi troops had already been in action for a long time. Fearing a loss of contact with all his friends, he returned to Germany for the duration of the war. By the time war ended he had lost many friends in Germany, France, Britain. Many of his possessions, including drawings, were destroyed in a fire. He was living in the Black Forest when his life took another turn, and he met a man who greatly admired his work and who was to help him financially for some twenty years.

In 1944 Alastair, now fifty-seven years old, was living in a small hotel room in Gernsbach. Among his closest friends were Frau Lily Schoeller, married to the heir to the Schoeller paper works, and now herself a doctor at the Genetic Institute in Freiburg; and Frau Waltraud Nicolas. Frau Nicolas was a journalist, wife of a communist journalist whom she had joined in Russia. He had been killed there in the aftermath of the Tukhachevsky affair, and she had spent four years in a prison camp, returning to

Germany after the signing of the Ribbentrop pact. She had written an anti-Soviet memoir, *Der Weg Ohne Grade*, which was published in 1943 after Germany's invasion of the Soviet Union. Her publisher had introduced her to Alastair. Alastair was also friendly with several people involved in the plot to assassinate Hitler.

Dr Hans Werhahn recalls his first meeting with Alastair in 1944. A member of a leading industrial family from Bonn, Werhahn was then a very young army conscript. Fascinated by what he had heard of the multi-talented Alastair, he put on his best civilian clothes to visit him. The first meeting proved extremely difficult: Alastair, seeing his visitor arrive in civilian clothes, took him for a Gestapo man, and was duly terrified.

Friendship survived this first meeting. Dr Werhahn was to provide the basic financial security for Alastair until the latter's death, and he and his wife helped look after him whenever needed.

The immediate post-war years were highly unsettled and nomadic for Alastair, who moved over and over again. He lived for a while in a charitable home for former servants in Constanz. It was run by nuns, and he there became friendly with Father Theophil Tschippke, a Dominican priest. Alastair had been a life-long epileptic, but his illness had always been controlled by drugs. During one of his moves he developed an extensive hernia caused by his lifting of heavy luggage. Because of his precarious health the doctor refused to operate, and in early 1948 he moved to an old people's home at Unkel, near Bonn. This, too, was run by nuns. (Though born a Protestant, he was eventually buried as a Catholic.) Dr Werhahn brought him to Bonn, where he stayed for a year before moving to Freiburg. From there he travelled from town to town, often staying with friends. In 1954, at last, Alastair moved to Munich, to the Haus Biederstein, the town house of Countess Harrach which she had converted into a residential hotel, where he had a pleasant two-room suite, as well as a studio in the attic.

From the late 1930s onwards Alastair had stopped drawing altogether. He continued to exercise his body until prevented by his hernia, and he continued silent finger exercises throughout the years when no piano was available. Most of his time was taken with translations. Another of his friends, Jakob Reisner, was a publisher. Reisner, who had studied art history and written a thesis on Kitsch, had first met Alastair in the mid-1930s. Eventually, Hermann Rinn was to publish a number of Alastair's translations in the post-war years. These did not pay very much, but the money supplemented his allowance from Dr Werhahn. Alastair translated over one hundred books from French and English into German, both prose and poetry, including works by Barbey d'Aurevilly, Baudelaire, Georges Bernanos, Léon Bloy, Paul Claudel, Marcelline Desbordes-Valmore, Gustave Flaubert, the tales of La Fontaine, Théophile Gautier, Mercedes de Gournay, Victor Hugo, Luc d'Estang, the Comtesse de Noailles, Stendhal, Robert Louis Stevenson, Bulwer-Lytton, Thackeray, Oscar Wilde, Rimbaud, Paul Valéry and Keats. Much of this extraordinary hard work was never published, including a twelve-volume translation of the *Histoire des Albigeois* . . .

He made several new friends, but rarely, if ever, left his rooms. Visitors arrived in the evenings, bearing his favourite flowers, roses, lilies, chrysanthemums, in white, yellow or purple – his rooms were, whenever possible, transformed into fragrant bowers. The walls were hung with lengths of fabrics: silks and satins, printed and plain, aerial and weighted. Whenever he could afford it he would order lengths of new prints, new fabrics, new colours. Some for draping, others for clothes which he designed himself. His suits were elaborate overalls, the weight of the trousers hung on the shoulder straps, as he could not bear any tightness around his waist because of his hernia. His beautiful shirts all had high collars, his coats were a variation on the Inverness. He invariably ordered dinners in advance, lavishing as much care on each as ever. When well he would receive his guest or guests stretched out on a couch, wearing one of his more elaborate costumes. Later in life he received his guests in bed, his harlequin face embedded in lace

I The Passionate Embrace.
'There is an intensity of rapture, an ecstasy, a frenzy of love at its climax, which is the pure frenzy of youth, where the Chevalier holds Manon in his arms, her nakedness emerging from an immensely swaying prismatic robe.' From *Manon Lescaut* (see pls 10–13).

II Baudelaire.
From *Red Skeletons* (see pls 7–9).
An invocation to the poet from Harry Crosby:
'Within my soul you've set your blackest flag
And made my disillusioned heart your tomb.'

III Anger.
One of the seven deadly sins in all his magnificence, holding two spiked balls aloft, his whole body dripping with blood. From *The Temptation of St Anthony* (see pls 52–61).

II

III

IV

and frills. Always mindful of his dignity, he was a King holding court. In the daytime, though, he cleaned his own rooms.

In 1964 Alastair began drawing again. During the last five years of his life he was to produce about one hundred and fifty finished drawings. Among these were two sets based on tales by Gustav Meyrink, *Mann auf der Flasche* (Man on the Bottle), which Alastair characteristically renamed *Mann in der Flasche* (Man in the Bottle) and *Bologneser Tränen* (The Bolognese Train), and a third set, *Jeux de Cirque* (Circus Games), which abandoned his usual literary inspiration and harked back to his very early interest in the circus and its performers. The style of his imagery remained unchanged, his control of line still permanent. Each drawing was a structure wrought in space, out of time – there are no shadows, no detail likely to mar the total decorative effect of the individual drawing. They are never illustrations, but illuminations. In the 1960s he began to exhibit again, in Rome and Munich, and interest in his drawings was growing again from Paris to New York. He flew to Paris for the first time in his life to attend the opening of an exhibition of his works. Bavarian Television accompanied him, filming him in the aeroplane and later editing the result with a visual montage in which his drawings appeared framed in the cabin windows. Three further programmes were made by Bavarian Television on Alastair. One was an impressionistic and somewhat surrealistic set of images, filmed during the exhibition of the Man in the Bottle drawings in a Munich gallery and accompanied by a specially composed musical sound track. The others were straightforward long interviews in which Alastair was filmed in his bed. He had by then developed a goitre on the right of his neck, but he consistently held up the long collar of his shirt to conceal this.

Alastair frequently wore a little makeup, highlighting his eyes and cheeks. His makeup was exaggerated for these interviews, with some obtrusive lipstick. The flavour, nevertheless, comes over, the malicious high-pitched speaking voice, the glitter of his eyes, the studied gesture. Curiously enough, his singing voice, a rich baritone, was completely unlike his speaking voice. His feelings of persecution were, however, also on the increase. He

believed himself a prisoner, resented those who helped him, thought his enemies were concealing the letters sent to him and destroying those he wrote. 'There are dangerous people trying to destroy me in a clever way, but I am fighting for my liberty,' he wrote in a telegram he sent to Caresse Crosby, with whom he had started corresponding again in December 1966. 'I am living a sort of nightmare – impossible to bear,' he wrote in May 1968. 'Two years ago I made up my mind to try and fight for my liberty. But it must be done in a way that cannot be detected by the person who kept me in a clever kind of custody.' He told one of his guests that he feared someone in England. One of his letters ended: 'surrounded with flowers and danger'. To an Italian art dealer he revealed, with many injunctions to silence, that he was an illegitimate son of King Edward VII.

When one of his exhibitions was over and the drawings had not been immediately returned to him, he asked two of his dearest friends to fly out to Rome and ensure their safe return. Several galleries approached him for exhibitions, but he was afraid they would steal his work. 'I am nearly eighty now,' he wrote Caresse. 'Externally not very changed it seems. Only forcé de rester allongé a good deal.' In another letter he wrote: 'If I have to stay in bed – it's a nice bed and flowers – flowers all around – only it hurts sometimes very much – but I never identify myself with any pains and try to jump them.'

In 1969 Caresse expressed the hope that she would soon see Alastair in Munich. They were never to meet again. Alastair died shortly before her projected arrival. 'Time is quite unreal,' he had written once, 'a stroll in false perspective.' One of his poems, written in 1927, reads:

> *I do not know wherefrom*
> *And not whereto*
> *I stand in guilt*
> *A strangeness barks around me*
> *On all sides*
> *Sparks what I do not want*
> *Asks what I never knew*
> *Oh! even sunrays paint*
> *Wet shadows in the sand*
> *Unlike the shadow in my former place*
> *Out of the chimneys riddles foreign smoke*
> *Behind the forest – heedless mountain goat –*
> *Waits love for me perhaps*
> *And children sing*
> *My long forgotten name.*

IV Ashtaroth.
Also known as Astarte, she was a fertility goddess and the mother goddess of the Canaanites and the Phoenicians. From *The Sphinx* (see pls 1–6).

The Sphinx

By Oscar Wilde. First published by John Lane in 1894, this was originally a youthful poem, later revised. An invocation to the Sphinx, the 'exquisite grotesque! half woman and half animal!', it brought in a multiplicity of Egyptian echoes in its heightened language.

1 'Or that young God, the Tyrian, who was more amorous than the dove of Ashtaroth.' This is one of many admiring references to beautiful young men in the poem.

2 'Or did you when the sun was set climb up the cactus-covered slope To meet your swarthy Ethiop whose body was of polished jet?'

30

3 'Sing to me of that odorous green Eve when crouching by the marge >
You heard from Adrian's gilded barge the laughter of Antinous.'

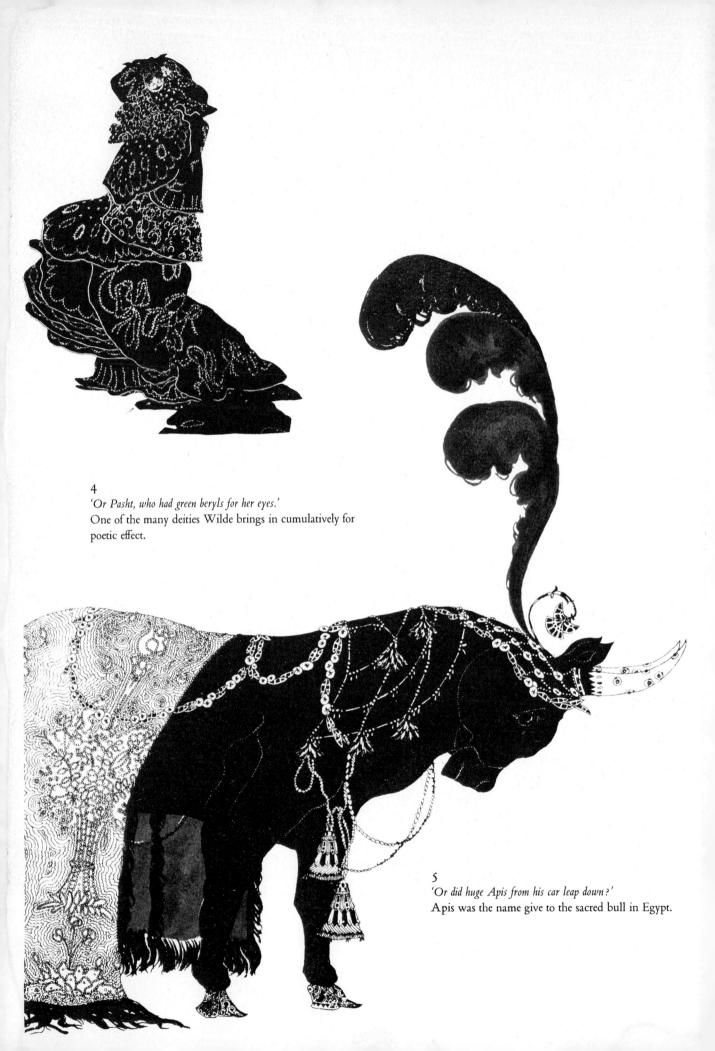

4

'Or Pasht, who had green beryls for her eyes.'
One of the many deities Wilde brings in cumulatively for
poetic effect.

5

'Or did huge Apis from his car leap down?'
Apis was the name give to the sacred bull in Egypt.

6

'Leave me to my crucifix,
Whose pallid burden, sick with pain, watches the world with wearied eyes,
And weeps for every soul that dies, and weeps for every soul in vain.'

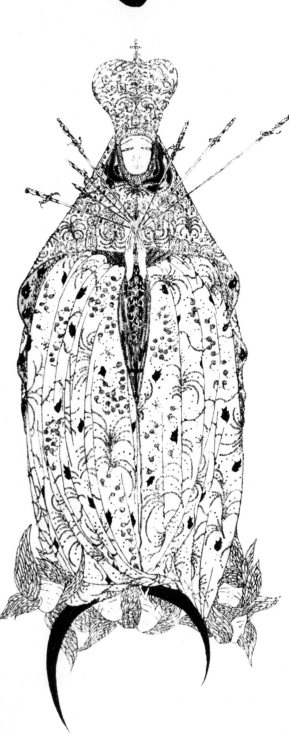

Red Skeletons

The first book published by Harry and Caresse Crosby under their imprint in Paris, it contained somewhat overheated decadent poems dedicated to Alastair.

7 Our Lady of Pain.
This was the subject of a poem by Swinburne, an image Alastair drew several times, equating her with the cruel moon-goddesses of Near Eastern mythologies. Swinburne, himself a masochist, wrote a moving invocation to her.

8 Cleopatra. This image, with its Egyptian lotus
blossoms, seems close to *The Sphinx* illustrations:
'With breasts uncurtained to the asp's red sting
I seek the death that Cleopatra died.'

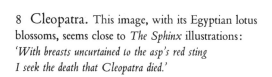

9 Salammbô. She was the heroine of a novel by Flaubert:
'Across black tiles the sacred python weaves,
Slips through her knees, along her moondrenched thighs,
Beneath her arms; oppressingly he cleaves,
Until his head is level with her eyes.'

Manon Lescaut

By the Abbé Prévost. First published in 1732, this novel traced the love affair of the Chevalier des Grieux and Manon Lescaut from their first chance meeting when she was on her way to a convent, through many vicissitudes, to her death in New Orleans. The notes are by Arthur Symons.

10 Departure.

'Manon's lover, dressed entirely in black, has seized her bodily, his haggard eyes close to her amorous face, pale cheek on pale cheek; her eyes are lewd and lascivious, her lips painted; she is garbed in some fabulous costume that whirls around her, scintillates, almost like a swirl of living serpents coiled inextricably.'

11 Disagreement.

'The insulter with his back turned to us, who has rudely entered her boudoir with the intention of exposing her perfidies, pointing to her lacquer cabinet, furiously, which contains the wanton's inevitable love-letters and laces and jewels and fans. She has turned her back on this Molière-like person, she is matchlessly dressed in a gown whose train sweeps the floor; her head bent over, one hand touching her hair and the other holding a half-opened fan, her face downcast, she, sure of the supremacy of her beauty, waits for more rampant curses from her Insulter. Does she repent? Having survived times out of number, will she ever repent?'

12 Chamber Music.
Manon and the Chevalier in their happiness after their
escape from prison.

13 At the Play.
Manon with M de B⸝ in a box at the theatre, 'where she
was so gorgeously dressed' (Prévost).

Sebastian van Storck

Walter Pater's tale of a Dutch burgomaster's son, resisting wealth and public office in favour of philosophical arguments in solitude; having cruelly rejected the girl who loved him in a natural and loyal manner by accusing her of a 'vulgar coarseness of character', he then lost his life in saving that of a child from drowning.

14

'And it was in the saving of this child that Sebastian had lost his life.'

15
'Sebastian van Storck, confessedly the most graceful
performer in all that skating multitude.'

16 The Chinese Parasol:
'the principled Présidente and the Vicomte'.

Les Liaisons Dangereuses

By Choderlos de Laclos. This classic eighteenth-century erotic novel, written in the form of letters exchanged by the protagonists, deals with two libertines, the Vicomte de Valmont and the Marquise de Merteuil, and their various enterprises to corrupt and seduce the innocent. Alastair, discussing the placing, described the illustrations to his publisher as belonging to the book 'by atmosphere and the persons – but not in a strict illustration of a scene described in the book'.

17 Passionate Embrace:
'the wicked Marquise and the touching lover'.

18 Bad Counsel.

19 The Insulting Bird

'is the girl and it would be good to put that drawing in where everything is going against her and she begins to be rather nervous'.

The Fall of the House of Usher

By Edgar Allan Poe. Alastair considered his usual fine-line inked technique too clear-cut for this heavily atmospheric short story, so he illustrated it with soft lead pencil drawings, carefully smudging and blurring the lines to produce greys and blacks, adding the occasional touch of red pencil to heighten some details.

21 Usher and Madeline.
The tragic, pallid faces of the doomed brother and sister, as trapped by their fate as a spider's victims caught in its web.

Carmen

Prosper Mérimée's tale of the love of a Spanish officer, Don Jose, for a cigarette factory girl, Carmen, for whom he abandons his fiancée and deserts the army. When his funds run low the fickle Carmen leaves him for Escamille, a bullfighter. The jealous Don Jose then stabs her to death. The story was later turned into an opera with music by Bizet. Alastair produced 12 illustrations for a German version of the tale, published in Zurich in 1920. These illustrations are from an earlier set, published in *Forty-Three Drawings* in 1914.

22 'Drôles de gens que ces gens là'
(Curious types, those people).

23 'Je t'aime, Escamille'.

24 'Ah je t'aime, Escamille'.

Salome

Alastair executed several sets of drawings to illustrate Oscar Wilde's play, originally written in French for Sarah Bernhardt, who was prevented from playing in it in London by the Lord Chamberlain, the theatre censor. The following drawings were reproduced in *Fifty Drawings by Alastair*. The drawings used in the *Salome* book published in Paris are different from these, though some are no more than variations.

25 Salome and Jokanaan.
The princess attempting to seduce the imprisoned and bound prophet, John the Baptist, called Jokanaan in the play.

26   Herod.
The king on his throne, watching his step-daughter,
Salome, dance for him after promising her anything, even
half his kingdom, to do so.

27 Herodias: 'My daughter has done well'.
Salome has demanded the head of Jokanaan, her mother's
greatest enemy.

28 Herodias.
Salome's mother, she has married King Herod, her former
husband's brother.

29 Salome:
about to kiss the lips on the severed head of Jokanaan, her
clothes, headdress and body streaked with his blood.

54   30 Salome and a Guard.

31 The death of Salome.
Still clutching the severed head of Jokanaan, she is
surrounded by guards who crush her with their shields.

32 Tosca and Cavaradossi.

La Tosca

The highly melodramatic tale of Floria Tosca, a celebrated singer, and her lover, the painter Cavaradossi, whose aid to Angelotti, an escaped political prisoner, allows them to fall into the hands of Scarpia, the Chief of Police. All the protagonists die in the end. Sardou's play was turned into an opera by Puccini.

33 Tosca and Scarpia.

34 The Execution of Cavaradossi.

35 The Secret.

La Dame aux Camélias

This almost perfect romantic novel by Alexandre
Dumas fils inspired an extended series of
delicately elegant drawings by Alastair, who may
have felt an affinity with the beautiful but
consumptive courtesan, Marguerite Gautier, who
sacrifices everything for love. These four drawings
were published in *Fifty Drawings* (1925).

36 Marguerite Gautier.

37 The Faint.

38 The Death.

The Blind Bow~Boy

By Carl Van Vechten. A modish, clever and
entertaining novel first published in 1923, it
recounts the adventures of Harold, a complete
innocent, at the hands of the sophisticated, bright
and wealthy folk of New York. 'The painter,
uncharacteristically, has followed the description
of the characters as it is set down in the novel,'
wrote Van Vechten, 'but he has done much more
than that. By employing curious symbols, he has
brought about an interrelation between the plates.
Admirably, then, as these drawings serve to
illustrate my book, they also excellently play an
independent drama of their own.' The Blind
Bow~Boy is Eros, the God of Love.

39 Harold:
'the attractive young man, with chestnut~coloured hair,
brown eyes, a healthy complexion, and a fairly competent
build', who 'looked well in his clothes . . . which any
sophisticated person could have told you came from a Fifth
Avenue tailor.' He marries Alice, leaves her, has a torrid
affair with Zimbule, and ends up with Ronald.

40 Campaspe
'was about thirty, intensely feminine, intensely feline, in the
most seductive sense of the word. She was addicted to chain
smoking, that is she lighted one cigarette from the other as
fast as it burned too near the end of her amethyst holder.'

Erdgeist

Alastair felt a close affinity with the sophisticated
world of Lulu as analysed by Wedekind in both
Erdgeist (Earth Spirit) and *Die Buchse der Pandora*
(Pandora's Box). He produced a dozen
illustrations for each of these for a German edition
which was published in about 1921; he also
produced a number of other drawings using
Erdgeist as a 'spring-board to send his fancy
winging into the ether' (Carl Van Vechten). The
drawings reproduced here come from his two
anthologies, and differ from the illustrations
published in the German volume.

41 Lascaris.

42 Skirt Dance.

43 Ballerina.

44 En Jockey (Dressed as a Jockey).

45 The Young Widow II.

46 The Young Widow I.

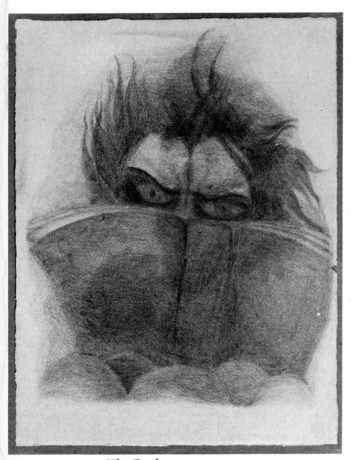

47 The Book.

48 The Mansion.

The City of Dreadful Night

By Francis Thompson. This mystical work by an American writer inspired a set of pencil drawings from Alastair more powerful than his *The Fall of the House of Usher* one. Executed in about 1929, these drawings just missed the era of luxurious illustrated books, and remained unpublished.

49 Night.

The Magic Flute

Mozart's masonic opera inspired several Alastair
drawings. With a libretto by Schikaneder, it
detailed the rivalry between Sarastro, representing
goodness and light, and his enemy, the Queen of
the Night, with a love story between Tamino and
Tamina and a comic love story between
Papageno and Papagena.

50 The Three Ladies.
Ladies in waiting to the Queen of the Night, they save
Tamino from a serpent and persuade him to rescue
Tamina, the Queen's daughter, from the hands of Sarastro.

51 The Queen of the Night.
She is here clearly seen as a moon-goddess, standing on a
crescent and with another crescent in her elaborate hair-do
which, with the multiple fans of her dress, houses the starry
firmament.

The Temptation of St Anthony

Alastair never succeeded in getting a separate book published of his many St Anthony drawings. This group was published in *Fifty Drawings by Alastair*. The parade of temptations, torments and horrors enabled Alastair to be considerably more fanciful than usual.

52 Reason and Logic.
A delicious conceit, worthy of Beardsley's *Bons Mots*; an epicene Reason forces Logic, a black clown, to dance on a
ball.

53 The Queen of Sheba, drawn by Dolphins.
One of the more appealing visions for the hermit.

54 The Indian Venus.
She dances with cymbals, accompanied by two monkeys
with castanets.

55 Sword Dancer.
The garlanded swords point their deadly steel at the svelte
dancer to form pure decoration.

56 The Poison Maker.

She is pure witch, her cat a familiar perched on her head.

57 Demons.

Combinations of fowl, insect, reptile, fish, beast and plant, these grotesques are more weird than frightening.

58 Demon.
A Hindu-inspired creation,
multi-headed, holding whips
and blood-dripping blades.

59 Prostitution.
A truly untempting vision of prostitution, raddled, over-made-up, yet with perfect firm breasts.

61 Crucifixion.
One of Alastair's recurrent themes, with a particularly blood-encrusted Christ surrounded by a highly dramatic grouping of the three Marys.

60 Three Blind Princes.
Reminiscent of the end of Marlowe's 'pampered jades of Asia', they are defeated, blinded, in chains.

Imaginary portraits and other illustrations

All but one of these drawings appeared in one or other of the Alastair anthologies, and are mostly inspired by poems or short stories. The exception is the *Dorian Gray* drawing, which was shown in several of Alastair's exhibitions in the twenties, including those in New York, Paris and Brussels.

62 Keats' Isabella.
She appears, of course, with her pot of basil.

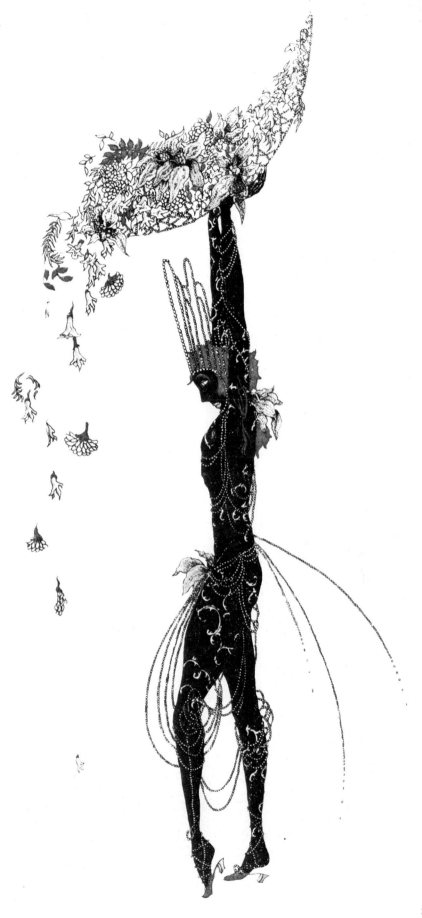

63 A Slave.

64 Paganini.
The legendary violinist, his music driving a woman to an
ecstatic swoon.

65 *L'Isle Joyeuse.*

66 *L'Oiseau peu Blessé.*

67 St Sebastian.

68 Messalina in Swinburne's *Masque of Queen Bershabe*.

70 Design for a Poster.

69 Design for Stage Costume.

71 *The Picture of Dorian Gray*.
Oscar Wilde's novel inspired several drawings by Alastair which are even more elaborate than usual. The tale of the young man who retained his youth and beauty while the image of his portrait aged and grew dissipated clearly appealed to him. This drawing represents Dorian Gray in Catherine de Medici's mourning bed.

Portraits

Alastair executed many portrait drawings of friends and personalities. The Bernhardt and Casati drawings in this section are from the author's collection. The rest are illustrated in *Forty-Three Drawings*.

72 Eleonora Duse.
Sarah Bernhardt's rival, La Duse, was both mistress and muse to Gabriele d'Annunzio, the Italian poet. Alastair was a frequent visitor at d'Annunzio's soirées in Paris throughout 1913.

73 Polaire.
The wasp-waisted actress who created the part of 'Claudine' on stage in Colette's play.

74 Mistinguett.
Miss was the star of the Casino de Paris music hall, and was to prove one of the most durable entertainers, showing off her famous legs until the 1950s.

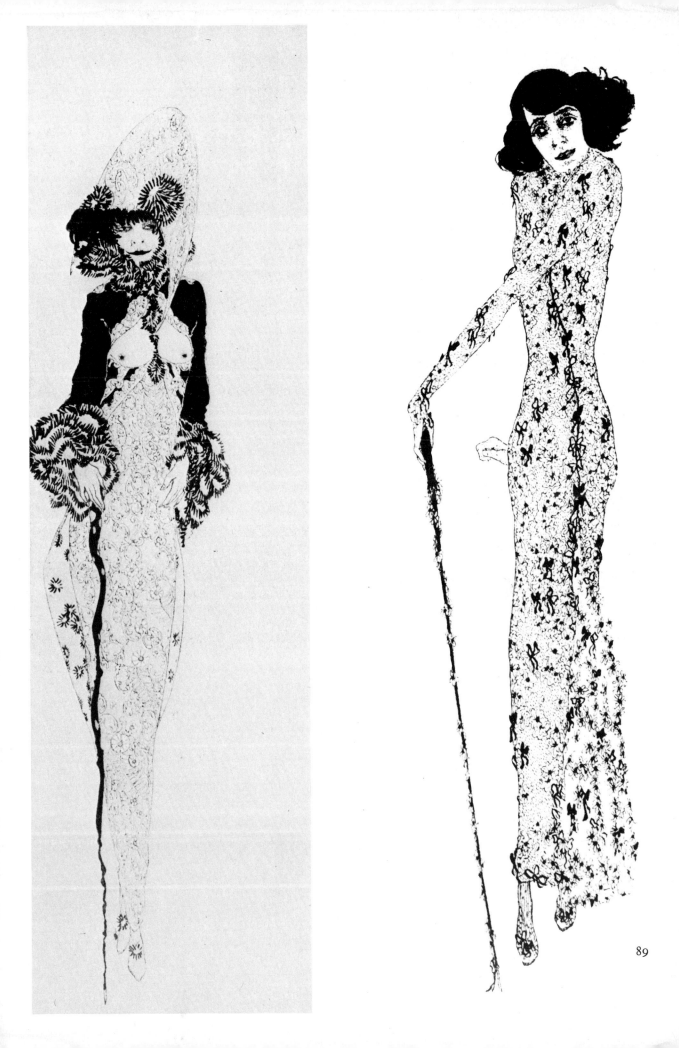

This was the overall title Alastair used for a set of drawings which explored the world of the circus, based on his youthful experiences when he had briefly joined one.

75 Marchesa Luisa Casati.
Alastair first met this extravagant *femme fatale* at one of d'Annunzio's parties; he found in her the embodiment of the theatrical he always sought.

76 Sarah Bernhardt.
She is shown here wearing a little feather ruff. Alastair was a great admirer of Sarah's, and always defended her as the finest actress of them all.

77 *Equilibre*
(Equilibrium).

78 *Nain-Dompteur et Chat en Fureur*
(Dwarf-tamer and furious cat).

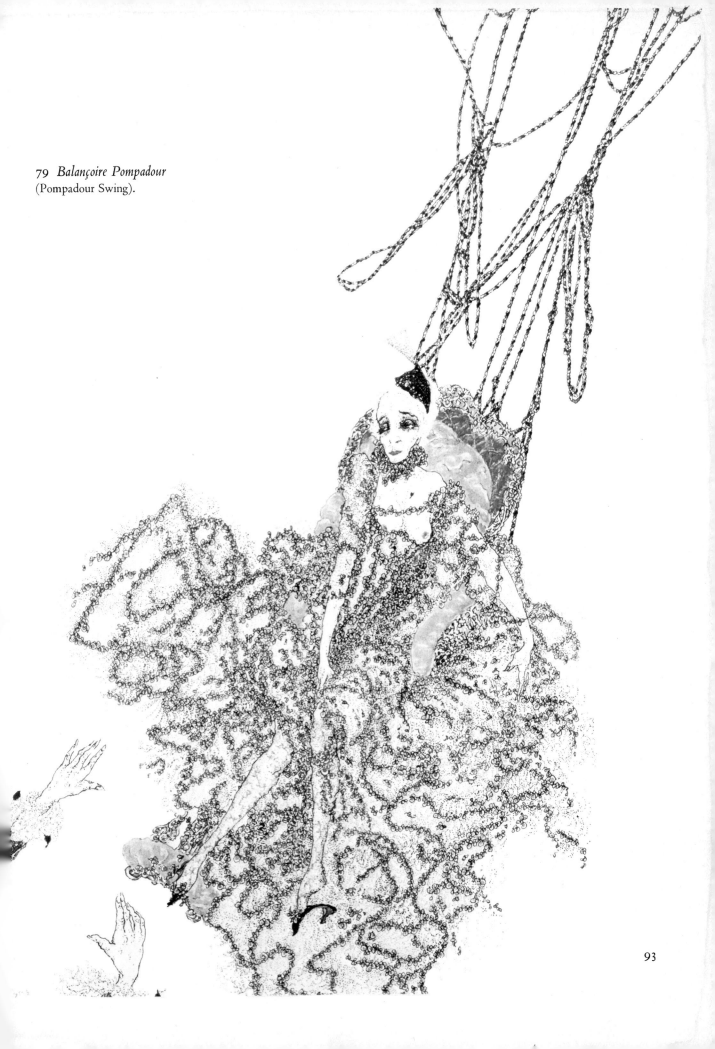

79 *Balançoire Pompadour*
(Pompadour Swing).

93

80 *Gestiefelter Kater* (Puss-in-Boots).

Der Mann auf der Flasche

This and *Bologneser Tränen* were fantastic tales by
Gustave Meyrink which inspired Alastair to
produce a large number of drawings, which he
started in 1964.

81 *Alraune* (Mandragora).
An illustration of the old legend of the manufactured
creature who became a *femme fatale*.

82 *Menschenfresser* (Cannibals).

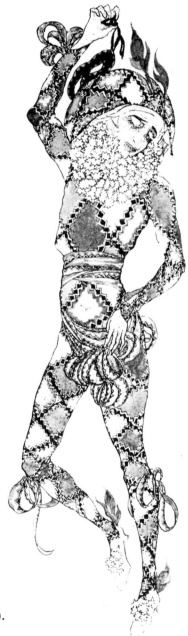

83 *Harlekin* (Harlequin).

84 *Schmetterling* (Butterfly).

85 *Scharfrichter und Schergen* (Executioner and aides).

86 From the Munich edition of Wedekind's
Erdgeist, *c.* 1921.

87 From the Munich edition of Wedekind's
Pandora's Box, *c.* 1921.

Acknowledgments

RETRACING the life of Alastair was a fascinating
exercise: parts of the puzzle appeared in Germany, the
United States, Great Britain, France and Switzerland.
I am particularly grateful to Dr and Mrs Hans
Werhahn for their great kindness, patience and
hospitality. They provided me with a vivid picture of
the later years of Alastair, as well as a number of
anecdotes and clarifications; they showed me many
Alastair mementoes, including some of his extravagant
clothes; and they made it possible for me to view the
television interviews Alastair recorded for Bavarian
Television. I am also greatly indebted to Professor
Kenneth W. Duckett, Curator of Special Collections
of the Morris Library at Southern Illinois University
for his considerable help in allowing me to consult
Alastair's letters, telegrams and other communications
to Harry and Caresse Crosby. Many people provided
some suggestions, information and clues, and
confirmed or denied others. They include Charlotte,
Gräfin Schulenburg, the Countess of Gowrie,
Ferdinand Neess, Godfrey Pilkington, Nourhan
Manoukian, Henry Ford and others who prefer to
remain anonymous: I am grateful to all of them, as
well as to Gretha Hamer for patiently deciphering my
scrawl and typing the text. With the exception of the
quotation from d'Annunzio's *Notturno*, all translations
in this book are mine.
I want to thank Phaidon Press Ltd for permission to
quote Stephen Hardman's translation of the passage
from Gabriele d'Annunzio's *Notturno*, published in
d'Annunzio by Philippe Jullian; the Estate of Carl
Van Vechten for permission to quote from Carl Van
Vechten's introduction to *Fifty Drawings by Alastair*,
published by Alfred A. Knopf in 1925, as well as
from his novel *The Blind Bow-Boy*, passages from
which were used in the captions of Alastair's
illustrations to that book; Editions Sun for permission
to quote from André Germain's *La Bourgeoisie qui
Brule: Propos d'un Témoin 1890–1940*; The Bodley
Head for permission to quote from Robert Ross's
introduction to *Forty-Three Drawings by Alastair*,
Arthur Symons' introduction to *Manon Lescaut* by the
Abbé Prevost, P. G. Konody's introduction to
Sebastian van Storck by Walter Pater and J. Lewis
May's *John Lane and the Nineties*; and Hulton Press
Ltd for permission to quote the entry on Alastair in
Edward Gordon Craig's *Index to the Story of My
Days, 1872–1907*.
I should like to express my gratitude to Dr Hans
Werhahn, Alastair's executor, for permission to
reproduce his drawings. Dr Werhahn also kindly
supplied the photographs of Alastair, as well as the
illustrations for plates 77 to 87. All other illustrations
are from drawings and books in the collections of the
author and Editions Graphiques Gallery, London.

Bibliography

1 Books illustrated by Alastair

Between 1905 and 1914 Alastair illustrated a few privately printed books and pamphlets. All these illustrations appeared anonymously.

1914 *Forty-Three Drawings by Alastair (with a note of Exclamation by Robert Ross)*. London and New York, John Lane; Toronto, Bell and Cockburn. Text in English; edition of 500 copies; 43 illustrations plus 1 endpaper design plus 1 cover design.

1915 *Poèmes pour Pâques* (Loïs Cendré). Geneva, privately printed. Text in French; 7 illustrations printed anonymously by 'Celui qui aime l'amour'.

1920 *The Sphinx* (Oscar Wilde). London, John Lane. Text in English; edition of 1000 copies; 10 illustrations plus 8 initial letters plus 2 endpaper designs plus cover design.

1920 *Carmen* (Prosper Mérimée). Zurich, Verlag Rascher u C. Text in German; edition of 500 copies, including 50 on Japon paper; 12 illustrations.

c.1921 *Die Buchse der Pandora* (Frank Wedekind). Munich, George Muller Verlag. Text in German; 12 illustrations plus 1 endpaper design.

c.1921 *Erdgeist* (Frank Wedekind). Munich, George Muller Verlag. Text in German; edition of 500 copies; 12 illustrations plus 1 endpaper design.

1924 *Die Rache einer Frau* (Barbey d'Aurevilly). Vienna. Text in German; 9 illustrations.

1924 *Sebastian van Storck* (Walter Pater). Vienna, Im Avalun Verlag. Text in German; edition of 480 copies; 8 illustrations.

1925 *Salome* (Oscar Wilde). Paris, G. Crès. Text in French; 9 illustrations.

1925 *Fifty Drawings by Alastair* (Introduction by Carl Van Vechten). New York, Alfred A. Knopf. Text in English; edition of 1025 copies; 50 illustrations.

1927 *Sebastian van Storck* (Walter Pater, Introduction by P. G. Konody). London, John Lane; New York, Dodd Mead & Co. Text in English; edition of 1050 copies; 8 illustrations, of which one is signed in pencil by the artist. These illustrations are identical to those in the 1924 Vienna edition.

1927 *Red Skeletons* (Harry Crosby). Paris, Editions Narcisse. Text in English; edition of 370 copies (including 33 copies on Imperial Japon paper), of which approximately 84 were destroyed by Harry Crosby; 9 illustrations.

1928 *The Fall of the House of Usher* (Edgar Allen Poe, Introduction by Arthur Symons). Paris, Editions Narcisse. Text in English; edition of 308 copies, including one on old Japon paper containing the original drawings; 5 illustrations.

1928 *L'Anniversaire de L'Infante* (Oscar Wilde). Paris, Black Sun Press. Text in French; 9 illustrations.

1928 *The Birthday of the Infanta* (Oscar Wilde, Introduction by Harry Crosby). Paris, Black Sun Press. Text in English; 9 illustrations.

1928 *Manon Lescaut* (Abbé Prévost, Introduction by Arthur Symons). London, John Lane; New York, Dodd Mead & Co. Text in English; edition of 1850 copies; 11 illustrations plus 2 endpapers plus dust wrapper.

1929 *Les Liaisons Dangereuses* (Choderlos de Laclos). 2 volumes. Paris, Black Sun Press. Text in English; edition of 1020 sets, including 15 on Japon paper; each volume has 7 illustrations.

1933 *Dangerous Acquaintances* (Choderlos de Laclos). New York, privately printed for William Godwin Inc. A very poor reprint of Vol. 1 of the Black Sun Press edition of *Les Liaisons Dangereuses*; 7 illustrations.

1933 *Manon Lescaut* (Abbé Prévost). New York, privately printed for Rarity Press. A very poor reprint of the John Lane edition; 7 illustrations.

1974 *Sebastian van Storck* (Walter Pater). Frankfurt am Main-Berlin-Vienna, Propyläen Verlag. A facsimile reprint of the 1924 Vienna edition; edition of 400 copies; 8 illustrations.

2 Other Works by Alastair

1920 *Das Flammende Tal*. Munich, Hyperion Verlag. Edition of 680. This was a volume of Alastair's poetry.

1922 *The Golden Hind*. Vol. 1, No. 1. London, Chapman and Hall. Illustration p. 34.

1923 *Ibid*. Vol. 1, No. 4. Illustrations pp. 8, 27.

1923 *Styl*. Vols 5/6. Berlin, Verlag Otto von Holten. *Die Verwandlungen des Dandy*. Article by Alastair with 7 illustrations.

1925 *Avatar* (Théophile Gautier). Hellerau bei Dresden, Avalun Verlag. This was Alastair's first published work of translation. Hermann Rinn published a number of Alastair translations in the 1950s.

Index

Italic numerals refer to black and white illustrations, roman I–IV to colour plates

ALAIN-FOURNIER 11
André, Edith 23
Andreae, Madame 9
Anning Bell, Robert 7
Atlantic Monthly, The 19
Auchincloss, Louis 17
Austen, John 13
BARBEY D'AUREVILLY, Jules 13, 24
Barjansky 5
Barrès 5
Bataille 5
Baudelaire 5, 17, 18, 24, *II*
Bax, Clifford 13
Bayen, Maurice 22–3
Beardsley, Aubrey 6, 7, 8, 11, 15
Bernanos, Georges 24
Bernhardt, Sarah 6, 16, *76*
Berry, Walter 17, 20
'Bianca' 10
Bibesco, Princess Marthe 17
Birthday of the Infanta, The 19
Black Sun Press 19, 21
Blind Bow-Boy, The 13, 15, 22, *39–40*
Bloy, Léon 24
Bodley Head, the 6, 7
Bologneser Tränen 29
Boyle, Kay 21
Bradshaw, Lawrence 13
Brimont, Renée de 23
Bulwer-Lytton 24
Camille see Dame aux Camélias, La
Carmen 7, 8, 12, 22, *22–4*
Carter, Frederick 13
Casals, Pablo 23
Casati, Marchesa Luisa 6, *75*
'Catherine' (Barjansky) 5, 6
Cendré, Loïs 12
Chabannes, Mme de 23
Chariot Of The Sun 19, 20
Chentoff, Polya 21
Chimay, Princesse de Caraman 23
Choderlos de Laclos 21
City of Dreadful Night, The 20, 23, *47–49*
Claudel, Paul 24
Cleopatra 6, 18, *8*
Cocteau, Jean 17
Colette 6
Cortot, Alfred 23
Cournos, John 6
Craig, Edward Gordon 6
Crane, Hart 21, 23

Crane, Walter 7
Crosby, Caresse 16–23, 29
Crosby, Harry 16–23
Dame aux Camélias, La 15, 20, *35–38*
d'Annunzio, Gabriele 5, 8
Davies, W. H. 13
Derleth, Ludwig 15
Desbordes-Valmore, Marcelline 24
Deslandes, Baroness Elsie 5
d'Estang, Luc 24
Dowson, Ernest 21
Duse, Eleonora 6, 16, 18, *72*
EDDY'S ART STUDIO 22
Editions Narcisse 18, 19
Erdgeist 7, 8, 15, *41–6, 86*
FAESI, Robert and Jenny 23
Fall of the House of Usher, The 19, 22, *21*
Flammende Tal, Das 15
Flaubert, Gustave 6, 11, 24
Fleischer, Dr Charles 15
Foch, Marshal 17
Forain 5
Form 13
Forty-Three Drawings 7
'GABRIELLE' 9–10
Gautier, Théophile 24
Geetere, Franz and May de 21
George, Stefan 15
Germain, André 8–12, 23
Gibbings, Robert 13
Goethe 8
Golden Hind, The 13
Gournay, Mercedes de 23, 24
Guilbert, Yvette 18
HARLAND, Henry 7
Harrach, Countess 24
Heiseler, Henry von 15
Heisenberg 23
Hemingway, Ernest 17
Histoire des Albigeois 24
Horen 15
House, Frank 23
Housman, Laurence 7
Hugo, Victor 24
Huxley, Aldous 15
Huysmans 11
IMAGE, Selwyn 7
Jeux de Cirque 29, *77–9*
Joyce, James 20, 21
KEATS 24
Kessler, Count Harry 6
Konody, P. G. 18
LA FONTAINE 24
Lane, John 6, 7, 8, 13, 15, 16, 18, 19, 20
Larnage, Mlle de 9, 10

Lasker-Schüler, Else 10
Lawrence, D. H. 20, 21
Le Fer de la Mothe, Madame 11
Lescaret, Roger 18
L'Herbier, Marcel 18
Liaisons Dangereuses, Les 21, *16–20*
'Lilith' 9
'Loulou' (Lou Andrea – Salome) 9–10
Lustheim, Schloss 12, 16
MACKEY, Haydn 13
MacLeish, Archibald 17, 21
Magic Flute, The 13, 22, *50–51*
Magnus, Maurice 6
Mann auf (in) der Flasche, Der 29, *80–5*
Manon Lescaut 15, 18, 20, 22, *10–13, I*
Marlborough, Duchess of 17
Marsden, Francis 13
Matisse, Henri 8
Matthews, Elkin 6
May, J. Lewis 5, 16
Mérimée, Prosper 6, 12
Meyrink, Gustav 29
Mistinguett 6, *74*
Moreau, Gustave 15
Morgan, J. P. 16, 23
NICOLAS, Frau Waltraud 23, 24
Noailles, Comtesse de 22, 23, 24
Noeggerath, Felix 5
Our Lady of Pain 6, 18, *7*
PAGANINI 6, 22, *64*
Pandora's Box 87
Parrish, Maxfield 7
Pasternak, Boris 5
Pater, Walter 19
Pennell, Joseph 7
Philpot, Glyn 13
Picasso, Pablo 8
Poe, Edgar Allen 19
Poèmes pour Pâques 12
Poiret, Paul 18
Polaire 6, *73*
Polignac, Armande de 23
Polignac, Duchesse de 10
Portrait of Dorian Gray, The 22, *71*
Red Skeletons 18, 20, 22, *7–9, II*
Reisner, Jakob 24
Revue Européenne, La 15
Ribblesdale, Lady 17
Ricketts, Charles 7
Rimbaud 17, 24

Rinn, Hermann 24
Rodo, Ludovic (Pissaro) 13
Ross, Robert 5, 7
Rossetti, Dante Gabriel 7, 8
Rothenstein, William 7
Rouvier, Jean 23
Rudolf, Archduke 6
SALLE, Duchesse de la 16
Salome 6, 13, 15, 22, *25–31*
Sardou, Victorien 6
Savoy, The 7
Schnitzler, Mrs Arthur 23
Schoeller, Frau Lilly 23
Sebastian van Storck 19, *14–15*
Shadows of the Sun 17
Shannon, Charles 7
Shelley, P. B. 17
Spare, Austin Osman 13
Sphinx, The 12, 13, *1–6, IV*
Steer, P. Wilson 7
Stendhal 24
Stevenson, Robert Louis 24
Strang, William 7
Styl 14
Swinburne 5, 6, 18
Symons, Arthur 7, 12, 18, 19, 20, 22
Temptation of St. Anthony, The 15, 20, 22, *52–61, III*
Tennyson, Alfred, Lord 8
Thackeray 24
Thompson, Francis 23
Tosca, La 15, *32–4*
Toulouse-Lautrec, Henri de 18
transition 20
Tschippke, Father Theophil 23
VALÉRY, Paul 17, 24
Van Vechten, Carl 13, 15
Vengeance d'une Femme, La 13, 22
Verlaine 17
Verwandlungen des Dandy, Die 14
Vetsera, Marie 6
Villiers de l'Isle-Adam 8
WEDEKIND, Frank 5, 6, 7, 15, 21
Weeks, Edward 19
Weizsäcker, Carl Friedrich Freiherr von 23
Werhahn, Dr Hans 23, 24
Weyhe Gallery 15
Wharton, Edith 17, 20
White, Gleeson 7
Wilde, Oscar 6, 7, 12, 13, 18, 19, 24
Yellow Book, The 7, 13
ZOLA, Emile 18